Passion

ANNE BRENNAN
AND JANICE BREWI

Passion for Life

*Lifelong Psychological
and Spiritual Growth*

CONTINUUM · NEW YORK

1999

The Continuum Publishing Company
370 Lexington Avenue
New York, NY 10017

Printed in the United States of America

Library of Congress Cataloging-in-Publication Data

Brennan, Anne.
   Passion for life : lifelong psychological and spiritual growth /
Anne Brennan and Janice Brewi.
      p.   cm.
   ISBN 0-8264-1181-9 (pbk. : alk. paper)
      1. Middle age—Psychological aspects.   2. Middle aged persons—
Psychology.   3. Aged—Psychology.   4. Spiritual life.
   I. Brewi, Janice.   II. Title.
   BF724.6B76   1999
   155.6'6—dc21   98-52093
                                                            CIP

Grateful acknowledgement is made to Coleman Barks and Maypop Books for permission to re-
print his translation of "The Guest House" from *The Essential Rumi;* to Kevin Danaher for his
story "The Magic Dot;" and to Peggy Guditus for her poetry and story.

"Vacillation" and "Sailing to Byzantium" by W. B. Yeats reprinted with the permission of Simon &
Schuster from *The Poems of W. B. Yeats: A New Edition,* edited by Richard J. Finneran. Copyright
1928, 1933 by Macmillan Publishing Company, renewed 1956 by Georgie Yeats and 1961 by
Bertha Georgie Yeats. Permission of A. P. Watt on behalf of Michael B. Yeats for lines from
"Vacillation" and "Sailing to Byzantium."

"Love after Love" from *Collected Poems 1948–1984* by Derek Walcott. Copyright © 1986 by
Derek Walcott. Reprinted by permission of Farrar, Straus & Giroux, Inc., and Faber and Faber,
London.

*For many years we have been training others
to facilitate **Mid-Life Directions Workshops for
Personal and Spiritual Growth and Long Life
Directions Workshops for Personal and Spiritual Growth.**
They are an international group of outstanding
professionals. We dedicate this book to these
Mid-Life Directions Certified Consultants
around the country and around the world.*

Contents

Preface   9

1 *Vital Involvement and Soul Making in a Long Life*   13
  Poet and Philosopher   13
  Long Life Gift of the Twentieth Century   17
  The Undiscovered Self   21
  Conscious Aging: An Invitation from the Greater Self   28

2 *Growing in All Four Stages of Life*   34
  Growing into the World   34
  Growing throughout the Whole Second Half of Life   38
  Four Women: Four Stages   51
  Spirit Receiving: Spirit Giving   54
  The Soul Is Always Young   61

3 *A Jungian Perspective: Insights for Long Life*   68
  Seasons of the Heart   68
  The Unconscious in Jung's Theory of Personality Development   70
  The Collective Unconscious: Gifts from the Inner Sea   75
  Models of Life Movement   78

4 *The Shadow as Gold*   *86*
   Know Thyself   86
   Unfinished Business   89
   All Growth Comes from the Unconscious   93
   The Conversion of Oscar Schindler and Zaccheus
      in the Gospel of Luke   96
   The Gold in the Shadow   99

5 *One Story, One Life: Past, Present, and Future*   *104*
   Secrets   104
   A Call to Remember   106
   The Story Continues   109
   Love and Forgiveness   112
   Take Down the Love Letters   115
   The Spiritual Significance of Synchronicity   120

6 *Staying Generative*   *125*
   The Virtue of Care—Contemplative Living   125
   Typology: A Key to New Growth and Creativity   133
   The Gift You Have Received, Give as a Gift   143
   Grandparenting   159
   The Magic Dot   163

Bibliography for Notes and Suggested Readings   *167*

Preface

In the twentieth century, we witnessed an evolutionary mutation: long life became ordinary. Our life expectancy doubled. Now in the twenty-first century, at the beginning of mid-life, a person can expect to live another whole life. The sphere of evolution in our times at the beginning of this third millennium is the biological, psychological, spiritual gift of a second lifetime.

Life is a journey in becoming human. Initiated at birth, and even before birth, this journey continues in childhood and in youth, in mid-life and in the mature years, and in death itself. Life is a pure gift from the Source of all life.

Life's second half is a wake-up time. An unexplored inner and outer world awaits us and demands our attention. These are the years for the exploration of our inner space. These are the years for reclaiming lost, unknown, unused, unconscious aspects of myself.

Here is an invitation to explore other worlds. This is the time for the longest stride of our souls. This ending of life's first half is an invitation to a new "generativety," a time for the new awakening, a passion for life, human and divine.

Our own unconscious personality is a creative bed of new life. This archetypal inner life is not dried up in mid-life or in the mature years but remains for each of us a source of new life, new growth, vitality, and passion. If at times the creative bed of life is dammed or blocked, the Self can engineer a breakthrough at any time, in sickness, in diminishments, even in dying itself. The personality is never set: this is our thesis. Change and development, refining and enlargement of the personality; emergence of dormant potentials can go on through the whole life span.

Each of us wants to develop his or her own unique art of living the precious decades of our life. No less precious are the decades given to us in this twenty-first century, the decades of a long life 50—60—70—80—90+. Passion for life can mature in the aging person. Passion for life in each of us can mirror the passion for life in the Creator of life.

Can we become architects of our own aging? Can we tune in to the great architect of our life story, of our being, the Self, God's image in me. Aging is not just something that happens to us. Aging is an opportunity for the greatest journey of all, the living of a full life in all the seasons and stages of life. Aging is an invitation to drink fully of the cup in all the decades of life, each with his or her own unique creative nectar and food for the Soul. For this kind of growing we are invited to participate fully in our living and in our dying. We are called to full consciousness and full participation in our daily life, without which there is no Soul making. This is an adventure that both demands and engenders passion for life.

Mid-life and the mature years are simply life's process of refining and regenerating a Soul. We are called to be explorers of all the mid-life peaks and valleys as well as the summit of the mature years. This is an invitation and a challenge to each of us to create a new paradigm for our own aging. In doing so we do not simply serve ourselves but we make an enormous contribution to the urgent task at this moment of history: redefining the aging process as an ongoing passion for life with lifelong psychological and spiritual growth.

In this book we share many stories of people striving to be architects of their own aging. We are grateful to all of them. Some are celebrities who may be surprised to find themselves in these pages. Others are ordinary people like ourselves who have crossed our path or entwined our lives. In many instances we have changed the names and details to assure the privacy of these individuals. But just as often, with their permission, we used the name of the persons who so generously can mirror for us some insight about growth in the second half of our lives. The theories of the great adult-developmental psychologists, as well as great spiritual traditions, are enfleshed in these stories.

It has been a joy to work with people in the organization of Mid-Life Directions for the past twenty years. We designed and presented the first Mid-Life Directions Workshop in 1978. In 1981, we founded and made Mid-Life Directions our full-time ministry. We are most grateful to the group of dynamic women to which we belong, the Sisters of Saint Joseph of Brentwood, New York, for their continued encouragement in this pioneer work that seemed to choose us.

In these twenty years we have met thousands of people longing for the fullness of life and wanting to explore the possibilities of growth in our Mid-Life Directions Programs for people 35 to 65-plus and in our Long Life Directions Programs for people 60 to 85-plus. We owe a debt of gratitude to all the participants of these workshops and retreats for all they have taught us. We remember one woman in her eighties thanking us after a workshop and saying, "Thank you for taking our lives seriously."

This is what we hope this book does for you. We want it to help you take these precious years of your life seriously. They are a pure gift of God.

We thank all the professionals whom we have trained to present Mid-Life Directions and Long Life Directions Programs. These men and women are helping themselves and others to become artisans of a long life. They are found across the United States and Canada, in England, Ireland, Rome, India, Africa, Australia, Singapore, and Malaysia, Thailand, the Philippines, and Newfoundland.

The fact that the workshops we designed for promoting personal and spiritual growth in the second half of life are being presented to participants in all these different cultures says something remarkable about the human-life cycle. We are all spirits en-fleshed in clay, placed upon this earth, living this glorious life, enjoying the different stages of our human journey despite all obstacles, struggling for wholeness, moving toward greater consciousness—union with ourselves and union with others. Our journey is a common one: childhood, youth, mid-life, the mature years. We celebrate this long life and in doing so we give praise to the Giver of life. May this twenty-first century find us moving in directions where we cherish even more all the stages of life and find ourselves becoming explorers and artisans of the Soul and of age itself. May we come to realize that we are truly brothers and sisters of a common humanity and a global community.

We would be remiss not to mention the special people, who are our comfort, support, and encouragement in life and in our work. Both blessed with large families, our sisters and brothers remain our life support. We thank Michael and Kathy Brennan, John and Patsy Brennan,

Maureen and Tom Hennessy, Eileen and Kevin Danaher, Jim Brennan and Kay Brennan as well as Claire and Michael Brewi, Grace and Bill Smith, Rita and Ed Brogan, and Barbara McFarrell.

Unique in their fidelity, love, and support is Janice's aunt and our good friend, Ann Travis, and each of our nieces and nephews. We cherish the women who share our life commitment of service and love to God and neighbor, and remain dear friends generous in their giving: Pat McDonnell, csj, Maryann Rogers, csj, Mary Shalley, csj, Margaret Raibaldi, csj, and Nora McNiff, csj. We are grateful to Pat and Peter Bosset. Mid-Life Directions has relied on the countless hours of dedicated volunteer service of special people Kevin Meneilly, Attorney at Law; Susan Keenan and Leo Yochim the Co-Directors of Mid-Life Directions Development; Beverly Moench, our administrative assistant; John Houlihan bookkeeper; and Ed McGinty, accountant. Without this generous giving to us personally and to the mission of Mid-Life Directions, we cannot imagine how Mid-Life Directions could have reached so many people or accomplished all it has in these twenty years.

Vital Involvement and
Soul Making in a Long Life

Poet and Philosopher

She was born Margaret Lynn. Peggy married Bill Guditus. Family life was the supreme priority for Peggy and Bill and they proceeded to have and to competently raise ten children. Theirs was a home of love and laughter. There were camping vacations and noisy wonderful celebrations. Today, the house in which they reared their family is a historic landmark on Long Island in New York. It is an old house filled with character. It creaks with history and its walls and floors speak of family life a century before the Guditus clan. Now, Bill is dead a few years, the children are off living their own lives, and Peggy has been reconstructing her life, continuing to live her story in her seventies.

A philosopher at heart, a poet by nature, Peggy only began writing poetry after Bill died. Peggy soon won the Catherine Currie Award for Poetry and her poems were published in *Taproot: A Journal of Older Writers* (Quigg, 1993, 22–23). Eventually a volume of her own poetry was published. Peggy had discovered that every loss in middle or later adulthood can serve to cause us to reach within, to tap inner resources, to awaken sleeping potentials, to liberate unconscious, dormant dimensions of the Self and to enrich the personality and the world. This mother of ten, and grandmother of more than twenty, was not content to see her children and grandchildren living out unique and varied personalities and gifts. She claimed her own new dimensions and directions in midlife, and again, in the later years. Peggy turned to poetry, at first, as a contemplative, as well as active way, of re-mem-ber-ing her story. She was engaged in putting her story together, once again. Her grieving heart, following Bill's death, invited her to recall her love story. Does her poem, "Kitchen Rendezvous," reveal the young married lovers, husband and wife creating supper together, as equals, anticipating the equality movements, or the fifty-year-olds relishing the joys of the "empty nest"?

KITCHEN RENDEZVOUS

The radio is playing
The room warm and cozy
"Do you want to do the soup
or the salad?"
He fills her wine glass.
Celery and carrots taste better
when he cooks them.
He chooses the soup. She knew he would.
She rinses the radishes, dries the lettuce.
He searches for the spices
at the back of the cupboard.
"I'll cut the onions for your salad."
She notices how tan he's getting.
"I like it when you wear a housedress."
She reaches for a cutting board.
They dance to a favorite song.
She stirs his soup.
He seasons her salad. Who can live on bread alone?

Peggy Guditus could never "live on bread alone." We cannot "live on bread alone." Peggy could not "live on bread alone" in young or middle adulthood. In her later years, Peggy still cannot "live on bread alone." No one can live on bread alone.

Her poem "Accent" reveals a person in later adult life, nourished by the love of yesterday but searching for and eager to taste fully the love of today. Her life experience taught her that each season of her life had had its own joys and its own sorrows. She wants to drink fully of today's cup. Peggy lately discovered the Poet and Philosopher in herself. Each of us has an archetypal Poet and Philosopher within ourselves, to churn our past life experiences and awaken us to the *present*. This is just one of the many unique gifts of later adult life. We may not become a published poet as Peggy did, but we must allow our inner poet to make poetry of our own story. It is our inner poet who can awaken us with a clarion call to become architects of our own aging process.

ACCENT

If I am not content
with the season in which I live
perhaps I have not learned how to live.

If the snow falls on my white head
rushes against my cheek,
bites,

then buries the bottom branches of the pine, why should I
wish for spring?
Or when spring comes,
time to look for hidden buds
and crocus heads,
should I think of raking errant leaves,
forsaking spring without a May Day crown?

Memories are for yesterday.
Dreams are for tomorrow.
But this day I will hold, twist, turn,
holding, twisting, turning each new day
until I find the magic in it.
Then I will go to a mountain
and help the sun rise.

The aging Peggy Lynn Guditus still drinks fully from her cup of life. She gives her family a great legacy.

The richness she found in family life never prevented her from reaching out to the larger community. Even as a busy wife, homemaker and mother, Peggy taught religion for her parish church. Weekly, as part of a parish religious education program, she gathered children from the neighborhood into her "at home religion class." Then, the organization and communication skills she used at home were exercised in the position of *area supervisor* as she took on the role of communicating with hundreds of parents and organizing religion teachers and classes for the parish children of a 2,500 family parish. At the same time, she continued to teach her own class.

In midlife, when most of Peggy's children were well on their own way to adulthood and some already out of the house, she reassessed her life and gifts and took a full-time job as an administrative assistant with many responsibilities that used her creativity. As a wage earner once again, Peggy found herself relating and acting in whole new ways as part of a large staff. Always having a strong sense of who she was, Peggy accepted challenge and change and used them to allow new aspects of herself to emerge.

Today, this woman in her seventies, widowed, retired from her administrative assistant position, recovering from cancer, continues to be generative as mother, grandmother, friend, poet, and philosopher. Her life journey has reached a peak in these last few years. The development of personality reflected in "Accent" is witness to the possibilities only a long life can bring. Peggy continues to be an explorer of "vital involvement in old age," not only for herself but for all of us. Peggy has passion for life.

Peggy continues to bear the tensions of the young/old polarity in herself. She both yields to the aging process and moves into the newness offered her. Still a child at heart, she embraces the joys and sorrows of the journey of life. She expresses in word and deed the wisdom this embrace brings to birth in her.

KALEIDOSCOPE

Peggy Guditus

I grow old
spouting discontent
like a smoldering
adolescent

searching for equanimity
beneath molting trees
and gardens that grow
beyond my reach

gathering ghosts
morning and night
while I look for the space
where awareness hides

who am I

If I plan a new journey
what shall I take
what shall I leave
must it be old
should it be new

then the answer
softly

take the sun
and the moon
remembered laughter
a pillow for your head
and a kettle
for the tea

Long Life Gift of the Twentieth Century

Today, we are not surprised that a woman in her seventies like Peggy Guditus, living at the dawn of the twenty-first century, has had a full, diversified life and is still exploring and discovering new creative aspects of herself in her later years. The twentieth century blew open the patriarchal exploitation of women who had been locked into the culture's definition of them. It also exposed the culture's debilitating bias regarding the nature and role of the older citizens. However, what most differentiates these two facts is this: the women we have always had with us, but the aged in such numbers is truly an evolutionary phenomenon of the twentieth and twenty-first century. Long life is the newest, unique, untapped resource, gift, and creative challenge of the twenty-first century.

When we hear of someone dying in their forties or fifties today, we are shocked. If death comes to those in their sixties, we have the sense that they were "so young"! There was so much ahead them! Even with someone dying in his or her seventies we question: how come, when so many others are living on into their eighties, nineties, and beyond?

We grieved to lose Jacqueline Kennedy Onassis and actress Audrey Hepburn, both in their sixties. So young! We mourned the tragic and premature death of thirty-six-year-old Diana, Princess of Wales.

As we prepared the first draft of this manuscript, a *New York Times* Sunday obituary page jumped out at us flashing the ages of the dead that week. Above the columns of minute death announcements, the editors featured the death of five public figures.

Dr. Bernard L. Osed, Biochemist, 95
P. H. Spencer, an Early Aviator, 97
Daryl Chapin, Codeveloper of the Solar Energy Cell, 88
James Bell, Expert on Plasticity, 80
Hans P. Nordheimer, Trade Executive, 88

Their advanced ages were a new and remarkable phenomenon of the twentieth century. Not only are people like this living this long, but many are doing so with individual style, continued "vital involvement," and passion for life above all: ongoing personality development and personal growth.

A recent art exhibit in New York City featured thirty older professional artists. All were found doing their most creative work when they were well into their sixties. The exhibit was titled: *Still Working.* Yet, already the idea of "Still Working" at sixty is unremarkable. Still working at seventy, eighty, or ninety is more true for the artists of this new century. We all know of wonderful achievements by people in the later years. Katharine Hepburn, the actress so noted for her wit, charm, and courage, received her fourth Academy Award for her leading role in *On Golden Pond*. She was seventy-four at the time. Gloria Stuart was nominated for an Academy Award in her eighty-seventh year for her role in *Titanic*.

Betty Friedan, an important figure of the twentieth century women's movement, had her groundbreaking book, *The Feminine Mystique*, published in 1963 when she was forty-two. Thirty years later, at seventy-two, after ten years of research on aging, and a bit of aging herself, she made another unique creative contribution in the publication of her book, *The Fountain of Age*. In her early book, she broke through the cultural stereotypes of who a woman is. In the *Fountain of Age*, she breaks through the cultural stereotypes of who the older person is. We are not at all surprised at people making significant contributions in their later years today, as Betty did. To prove the point, she published yet another book, at seventy-seven, *Beyond Gender*. At seventy-seven, senator and astronaut John Glenn took his second voyage into outer space, thirty-six years after his first voyage.

Yet, at the beginning of the twentieth century, in 1900, the average life span expectancy was forty-seven. We find this hard to believe, no less to comprehend. Recently, we were stunned when we heard this statistic on the radio: "Seventy-five percent of all the people who have ever lived to be sixty-five are alive at this very time." We are dumbfounded by statistics like this. This increased life expectancy is a great challenge and opportunity for each of us as individuals, as well as culturally, for our nation and for the world. Is it possible that the life span has increased at the moment in human history when humans and humanity itself were ready for this greater longevity? What if we were not to accept this invitation to greater longevity through mass suicide or genocide? What if failing to have hope in the maturation and gifts that a long life holds out to us, we fought with all our strength to resist aging and hold on to youth? What terrible value have we placed upon youth and what disrespect for age, that so many of us in the "second half" of life want only to feel young, look young, act young, be young?

Still, it is true that, *"The soul is always young."* In these soul-making years of midlife and old age, someone's soul and spirit can soar, as it never did in childhood and youth, giving him or her an openness, vitality, eagerness for life, a childlike contentment and creativity beautiful to behold. Maturation, in these years, can so enliven the spirit that even in the physical deterioration that comes to some in advanced old age, the spirit, free at last of neurotic compulsions or clinging materialism, can give witness to a blessed solidarity with self, others, and nature—all shot through with grace and spirit.

In the twentieth century, we witnessed an evolutionary mutation, long life became ordinary. Our life expectancy doubled. Now, in the twenty-first century, at the beginning of midlife, a person can expect to live another whole life. Yes, history reveals rare people who lived to be seventy, eighty, or ninety; yet, in the first half of the twentieth century and prior to that, fifty- and sixty-year-olds were considered ancient. Only a rare few lived beyond their sixties. Today, it has become commonplace to be over sixty, over eighty, ninety something. Carl Gustav Jung, the Father of Adult Developmental Psychology, who died himself at eighty-six in 1961, said, "Whoever carries over into the afternoon the law of the morning—that is, the aims of nature—must pay for so doing with damage to his (or her) soul . . . a human being would certainly not grow to be seventy or eighty years old (and we add ninety and a hundred to this) if the longevity had no meaning for the species to which s/he belongs" (Jung, 1933:109).

Jung had very creative insights about the meaning of long life for the species. Long life is for wholeness, personality development, growth in consciousness, individuation, and for the culture. There is personality development that can and should go on in the midlife years and in the later adult years, which can take place only with a length of years. Old age is for inner and outer development, not for decline.

Even the unavoidable disintegration and diminishments of aging and dying are for development. The human development possible only in later adult life is not just for the individual, it is for the culture. This evolutionary mutation is to be harnessed. Society desperately needs what only age can bring, but does not necessarily bring: wisdom. Speaking of wisdom and old age to Daniel Goleman, Joan Erikson said, "Lots of old people don't get wise, but you don't get wise unless you age." The biblical book of Job also saw a connection between aging and wisdom, "With age there is wisdom, and many years bring insight" (Job 12:12).

It is the task of this twenty-first century to promote the growth and gifts of the older generations and to harness the wisdom to which the culture has been oblivious and has denied and wasted up to now. We are each challenged to enter into creating a new paradigm for our own aging. As more and more individuals do this, we will each be making a contribution to the urgent task at this moment of history: redefining the aging process as ongoing passion for life with lifelong psychological and spiritual growth.

This we do know: aging is for soul making. Aging is for the growth and becoming of the magnificent human spirit. It is a spiritual enterprise, a godly thing.

The Undiscovered Self

Expecting to live on in our sixties, seventies, and eighties and beyond, we each ask the question for ourselves personally—and for our nation as a whole, even for the world—what is later midlife and old age for? What is the significance for the individual, and for culture of an expected life span beyond fifty or better beyond seventy?

To explore this question, our individual and collective psyche must break through the cultural prejudices of ageism. As each forty- or fifty-year-old comes to delight in the possibilities of midlife growth and finds the new dynamism inherent in life's second half, he or she starts on the second journey. It is a journey filled with more potential for personal and spiritual development than one could ever have imagined. Life's greatest accomplishments and most creative achievements can come from people in life's second half. As we approach each new decade of life, with its startling new awakenings, we are invited to explore new dimensions of self, and enter into the unique development of character and personality called for by that decade. This is the becoming of the Self, the Wisdom, and the making of a Soul, which only increased years can bring.

Martha Graham, one of the greatest pioneers of modern dance in America, was sixty when she realized that her dancing days were over. Martha had identified herself with her dancing. She was a *dancer*. Consciously or unconsciously, she could not imagine her life without dancing. At the same time as Martha was dealing with the end of her dancing days, and asking the question, "What am I going to do when I can't dance anymore?" she became sick and was hospitalized. As the doctors tried desperately to diagnose what was causing her to fail, she actually became semicomatose. In that place of nowhere, having nothing to live for, Martha existed, like Jonah in the belly of the whale. One day an answer, to her unspoken question came from her own inner depths. "Martha, Martha, if you cannot dance, why not teach other young people to dance?" From that day, Martha started to recover. Her own unconscious had given her a reason to live. Peggy Guditus found the *Poet* within herself, Martha Graham found the *Teacher* within herself. Martha founded the Martha Graham School of Dance. The TEACHER and CHOREOGRAPHER in her introduced Martha to her most creative years, which only ended with her death at ninety-seven. Today, her School of Dance continues in her wonderful tradition.

Erik and Joan Erikson are the developmentalists known for their life's work of exploring the human life cycle. In 1950, in response to an invitation, they went to the White House Conference and presented their life cycle theory at a midcentury convocation on human development. Years later, when Erik turned seventy, and entered his own eighth decade, the magazine, *Psychology Today,* featured him on the cover and carried an interview with the octogenarian. There, he confirmed with his own experience the life cycle theory that he and Joan made popular as a young man and woman.

Born in Germany at the start of the twentieth century (1902), Erik trained under Freud in Vienna, coming to the United States in the nineteen thirties. This psychoanalyst, author, theorist, and educator taught at Harvard, Yale and other leading universities. His wife, Joan, was his collaborator and editor.

In 1969, he authored the pioneering, prize-winning psychohistorical biography, *Gandhi's Truth.* He was a nondogmatic and creative Freudian. Once, when one of our mentors suggested we go to speak to the Eriksons about our work on midlife, we said, "How could we do that? We are so Jungian and they are Freudian?" "Not at all," our mentor, who knew the Eriksons personally, said, "They would enjoy and appreciate hearing about what you are doing."

Erikson went beyond Sigmund Freud's notion that the personality is decisively formed once and forever in early childhood. He asserted that the ego and its sense of identity go through a succession of crucial stages over a lifetime. He saw that psychosocial dynamics effect the resolution of each crisis and he pioneered new relationships between psychoanalysis and the social sciences. The work of Joan and Erik Erikson has helped us to see the whole life cycle as a progression of developmental stages. Because of their work, we have come to realize in a more powerful way that midlife and old age are developmental stages in their own right and not just pitiful endings tied on to a bright, energetic youth. His death, in 1994 at ninety-two, came after he had lived a full life, and he had creatively met the challenges that he encountered in his own aging process.

Well into his eighties, Erik, with Joan and a colleague, Helen Kiver, authored a book called *Vital Involvement in Old Age*. This was the first time Joan's name was included as the coauthor with her husband's name. Two years later, Joan authored her own book, *Wisdom and the Senses*. It was the first time she authored a book by herself with her own name as author. This reflects marvelous ongoing development of personality in these two adults in their eighties. It is interesting to speculate about what went on at this time in this marriage with these two lifetime companions and colleagues.

Joan had always participated behind the scenes, the hidden collaborator. Yet, now in her mature years, she finally blossoms forth, first as recognized coauthor and then as author in her own right. Kenneth Woodward tells us that, "Although their friends long recognized Joan as Erik's close collaborator in his research, and as editor of all his writings, her husband was anxious toward the close of his writing life to acknowledge the intimate weaving of her work with his" (6–8). The personality is not set. Change and development can go on all through life and in later adult life.

The Eriksons both lived *Vital Involvement in Old Age*. It was when the Eriksons lived in Tiburon, California, and we were studying in San Anselmo, California, that we were urged to go to see the Eriksons. Unfortunately, we let the opportunity pass. Years later, we were in the Bay area again and ventured to make that visit only to find that Erik was ill at the time.

In his later years, Erik was allowing undeveloped aspects of his own personality to emerge. He engaged a professor of Greek to teach him the language so that he could enjoy reading the New Testament Scripture in their original language. At that time, he also belonged to a men's prayer group that met regularly to pray and foster spiritual development. This was "Vital Involvement in Old Age."

Throughout life, and sometimes in our old age, we are asked to make concessions. Knowing when that time comes and making the necessary concessions is part of the maturation process. The day came when Joan and Erik decided to leave Tiburon behind and return to the Cambridge area near Boston where their children and grandchildren lived. They felt the desire and need to be closer to them as they came closer to the end of their ninth decade. At each stage of life, with each new moment, we relearn life's earlier lessons, as well as the challenging new ones. Joan and Erik reworked for themselves at this new juncture the "interdependence" so necessary for a fruitful life and for maturation.

The Eriksons' new life in Massachusetts was a creative one. They moved into a rambling, three-story Victorian house and took in boarders, so that they could have lively conversations. Their first three boarders were: a graduate student, a professor of comparative religion, and a psychologist. Living communally at their age was a whole new adventure for the Eriksons. There is no doubt that they were living examples of "vital involvement in old age," as well as examples of ongoing personality development in and through the mature years. We owe a debt to Joan and Erik Erikson for their work and for the models of long life that they are to each of us.

In the last decade of the twentieth century, two phenomenal women in their hundreds, Bessie and Sadie Delany, wrote a book sharing with us their experiences of a century of living. Always storytellers, in their hundreds they became published authors and witnesses of their own "vital involvement in old age," and passion for life.

Their father, born a slave, was freed by Lincoln and was elected in 1918 to be the Episcopal Church, U.S.A.'s, first black bishop. The Delany story is not only a personal story of two remarkable women, but also a unique story of American history. Furthermore, for each of us so interested in the phenomenon of aging in life's second half, it is a remarkable account of two women, "loving, laughing and embracing life after one hundred years of living side by side."

Their story, which was also a chronicle of American History, became a best-seller. Two years later, *Having Our Say: The Delany Sisters' First 100 Years* was adapted for the stage, opening in Princeton, New Jersey, and then on Broadway in New York.

Bessie's fire and spirit helped her become Harlem's second woman dentist and Sadie's quiet determination made her a teacher in the country's largest school system in New York City. The book and play are filled with golden nuggets for our own aging and for the long life with which we are blessed.

Following the opening of the play on Broadway, which they attended, Bessie celebrated her 104th birthday on September 3, and died on September 25, 1995. Speaking of her younger sister, Sadie said, "She had a ball these last two years [102–104!]. She loved all the excitement and notoriety of being a published author and then in May attending a performance of *Having Our Say* on Broadway."

Still keeping house by themselves and doing their own shopping and banking, they had a daily routine that included prayer and yoga. Fiercely involved with and loving the many members of their extended family, these two unmarried women in their hundreds opened themselves to yet another avenue of growth and development and became authors at 102 and 104 respectively. They became "American Treasures" and their story will be read in the decades to come in a book that is already an American classic.

The years following Bessie's death, Sadie authored another book, *On My Own at 107: Reflections on Life without Bessie.* "I never thought I could live without you," Sadie writes, "but here I am, like it or not. . . . I'm charting new ground, Bessie." Sadie's book quotes the Psalms.

> Planted in the house of Yahweh,
> they will flourish in the courts of our God,
> still bearing fruit in old age,
> still remaining fresh and green.
> Psalms 92:13–14

Sadie's book is largely a conversation with Bessie. She reveals herself at 107 to be a woman participating in her grieving, participating in her living. "This being alone," she tells Bessie, "is hard. For the first time in my life, I don't have you by my side. I'm 107 years old now, and it's like I'm just learning how to walk" (1997:6).

Sadie intuitively did some creative grieving for Bessie. "A few days after you left us, Bessie, I started wearing one of your suitcoats—you know, the gray one you loved so much. It made me feel good, having it wrapped around me" (1997:12).

Later she confesses, "I'm learning that I'm a separate human being. For the first time in my life, I'm learning that" (1997:20).

Religious faith was deeply rooted in the Delany clan and Bessie and Sadie, in their old age, made prayer a daily part of their life. Every human person has deep spiritual roots and our shared human history blesses us with a spiritual heritage we each need to learn to claim. Sadie found comfort in the Hebrew Scripture book of Isaiah, 46:4.

> "Till you grow old I am He [She]
> and when white hairs come, I will carry you still;
> I have made you and I will bare the burden,
> I will carry you and bring you to safety."

Sadie's religious faith was not only expressed in a prayer life but in living prayer. Sadie expressed her faith in her attitude toward life. An attitude toward life can be a living prayer. At 107, for Sadie, life was still a gift from God to be fully lived and cherished. The last line of her book is her testament to life and one that each of us could emulate: "I've got plans." Speaking to Bessie, she says, "Don't worry about me. . . . Child, I've got plans." Sadie has become a modern-day heroine. At 107, she is a pathfinder for herself and for each of us, for the human race, living life to the fullest even in the midst of profound grief. She continues meeting new challenges, growing and developing in a most remarkable way. Sadie Delany, *On My Own at 107: Charting New Ground*.

The same year that Sadie's book was published, the president of the United States of America appointed the eminent senior historian, John Hope Franklin, as the chairman of the Presidential Commission on Race Relations. Called out of retirement, this elder, John Hope Franklin, chose to accept the challenge to educate the country about race and about the past and convince its citizens to be proactive and to do more to make America "a nation undivided." He was called to challenge the nation to confront three hundred years of history and to promote racial reconciliation. In his mature years, Franklin was "charting new ground for himself," and hopefully, for the nation. Citizens Bessie and Sadie Delany had done some of the groundwork for him.

Without naming this man, let us share something of the story of a man in his eighties. This man had accomplished much in his fifties and sixties. A revered Roman Catholic clergy person, an author, he had an honored and respected key position. A noted spiritual leader and renowned speaker, he was a frequent guest lecturer throughout his diocese and nationally. As he moved out of his key position, he became a pastor where he focused his creative gifts tending a large parish with a rather large staff. Now, as a "retired pastor," a whole new life of opportunity has opened up before him. The willingness to change and explore the undiscovered and undeveloped self is as essential to the eighty- and ninety-year-old, as well as to the fifty-, sixty-, and seventy-year-old.

Giving a homily at a liturgy he celebrated for one of our programs, Monsignor shared with all of us some of his own recent experiences of change and development. He went weekly to a house of prayer staffed by a few nuns. One young sister teaches centering prayer, an imageless prayer style, familiar in mystical traditions of East and West. Monsignor can be found in her class, exploring and practicing this ancient prayer style, which is for him a new way of praying. Forty years ago, he taught hundreds of young people to pray and lectured on prayer and spirituality. Today, he can still teach us about prayer. Yet, he himself can still learn about prayer from a young woman old enough to be his grandchild.

Schooled in a time when priests and ministers did not fraternize with the laity, especially people in their parish, Monsignor had long ago moved beyond that "taboo" that had helped him to develop in his earlier days. When a dying parishioner asked him to pledge to be *Father* to his adolescent children and watch over them, this lifelong celibate gave his promise and lived it out. Frequent visits to these teenagers opened up new avenues and challenges. You can find on any day, a relaxed, eighty-year-old delighting in a new experience and adventure for himself: spooning food into an infant's mouth during a visit to one of these new mothers or fathers.

This achievement will not be listed in his obituary, but it is no small thing for this lifelong intellectual celibate. The journey of a soul is going on in these later years in strikingly human ways. The development of personality going on in him is not just for himself. He has become the elder of his tribe. The human race can look to him at this turning point for the guidance of someone who has continued to grow and become in his eighties. Having witnessed nine decades of church and national life and grown himself in each decade, he can address us at this turning in history. What is the span of eighty and ninety years for? It is for growth and development, the flowering of the personality, wholeness, generativity, wisdom, soul making, culture. Humanity desperately needs this evolutionary development.

Peggy Guditus, Martha Graham, Joan and Erik Erikson, Bessie and Sadie Delany, John Hope Franklin, and our aging Monsignor are living proof that aging is about a willingness to change. Aging is about continued growth and development. It is about nurturing inner awakenings and accepting new challenges brought on by the aging process. It is about new awakenings brought on by inner resources that become freed up in new and challenging circumstances. All this is part of a spirituality of aging. Aging has proved to us that each of us has not one adulthood. We each live through many adulthoods in this Long Life we have as a gift.

Conscious Aging:
An Invitation from the Greater Self

Developmental psychology is a science of the twentieth century. It is still not totally accepted. You can find learned and unlearned people who deny "adult" development in particular. It was Carl G. Jung who presented us with the life cycle in four stages: childhood, youth, midlife, and old age. In writing and teaching, we prefer to call his stage of old age the *mature years.* Jung's descriptive essay on the four stages of life is found in *Modern Man in Search of a Soul.* Surely today, he would have called it *The Modern Man and Woman in Search of a Soul.*

When we started our work on midlife and the mature years, we looked to the work of the developmentalists, the word of Erik and Joan Erikson, and in particular the psychology of Carl Gustav Jung. We favored Jungian psychology because it is primarily a second half of life psychology. We found that Jung's theory of personality helped the midlife person, as well as the person in the mature years, make sense out of the experience that he or she was having. Furthermore, Jung's psychology is open to the spiritual dimension of the person. He saw the religious function and the spiritual aspect of life as the very component that makes us most human. Freud taught us that our sexuality was repressed. Jung awakened us to our repressed spirituality.

We agreed with Dr. Jung that the midlife crisis was a crisis of meaning and so, at its core, it was a spiritual crisis. We soon learned in working with midlife groups that the midlife stage, which can be three or four decades of a person's life, is far more than the initial midlife crisis/transition. There is an early midlife, a middle midlife, and a later midlife stage, within the stage, each with its own spiritual as well as psychological growth.

Back then the words, "old age" had such terrible press that we decided to rename it, "the mature years," and to try to generate a new image for this last of the four stages of life. Everything is in a name, you know!

Robert Browning's words found in his poem "Rabbi ben Ezra," reflects the same vision, regenerating the very core and centrality of aging itself. It also incorporates all Jung's concepts regarding both midlife and old age. With poetic license, we can each consider the poem a hymn of our own Greater Self, our own soul to each of us.

> Grow old along with me!
> The best is yet to be,
> The last of life for which the first was made.
> Our times are in his hand
> Who saith, "A whole I planned;
> Youth shows but half. Trust God; see all, nor
> be afraid."

Notice that Browning's poem says: *"grow old."* He does not say, suffer heroically, or at least stoically, the inevitable decline of aging. He does not call us to accept and surrender to the inescapable: deterioration, decline, loneliness, and nothingness. He calls us to *grow* in our aging process. The poem invites us to *grow* in and through these natural stages of life. To grow in our aging calls for a full, active, and conscious nurturing and participation on our part. Browning's poem pipes a new song. This is a time for development, for a new blossoming, only possible at this time of life. We are each called to participate in conscious aging.

The older person in midlife and the mature years like the younger one, can look at the past years and ask, "How did I grow last year?" Looking ahead to a new year s/he can ask and wonder, "How will I grow this year?" That growth may be subtle or dramatic, but each fragment contributes to the whole. Writing in his autobiography, *Memories, Dreams, Reflections,* Jung speaks about the subtle growth in old age. "This is old age and a limitation. Yet, there is so much that fills me: plants, animals, clouds, day and night, and the eternal in man (and woman). The more uncertain I have felt about myself, the more there has grown up in me a feeling of kinship with all things" (1933:359).

As we read Browning's poem, we are invited to a meditation on this greatest of all adventures: the human journey. Life is a journey in becoming human. Initiated at birth, this journey continues in childhood and in youth, in midlife, in the mature years and in death itself. From a faith and spiritual perspective, we understand life as a *gift given* no matter how we perceive the Giver.

The poem reads, "*Grow* old along with me! The best is yet to be." It sees the "best" is ahead for each of us. What is this best? This "best" is not always found in length of years, but as Erikson said, it cannot be found without length of years. What is this "pearl of great price" buried in the process of "growing old?"

Jung understood childhood and youth as the time for ego development; midlife and the mature years for the development of the Self. To understand the significance of Browning's poem, one would do well to read it as an invitation from the Self. It is not the poet Browning who invites us to, "*grow* old along with me." It is our own greater inner Poet, the greater Self, our own Soul, the person we are still in the process of becoming, who gives us this invitation to come, "*Grow* old along with me!"

The Self connects us to our own "ground of being." The Self, the Soul, is both newborn and ancient at the same time. Newborn, because evolution into the greater Self is in process; ancient because the central core aspect of the Self is connected to God, to all humanity, to all creation, through and beyond time and space. So, it is our own ancient Guide and Poet who bids each of us, "Grow old along with *me!*"

What greater comfort could one ask for? "I am not alone." Another English poet, John Donne, told us "No man is an island."

No man stands alone. No woman is an island, no woman stands alone. A contemporary poet and songwriter tells us, "You are not alone. No one is alone." This human odyssey is not a lonely journey on which each of us embarks. Each of us is accompanied, led by the Self. And the Self, our Soul assures us that "the best is yet to be."

What is the best? The portion of life that is the last. This is because the second half of life is about a marriage. It is about the union of opposites within us. It is about becoming whole, becoming one. It calls for the final acceptance and integration of diverse parts of oneself. This is an inner wedding and an outer one. In the second century, Irenaeus said, "The glory of God is the human person fully alive." Jung called this, "individuation," that is, becoming all you are called to be; the making of a great soul, the becoming of the Self.

This is an archetypal journey made by others before us. The great, popular anthropologist, Joseph Campbell, instructed us regarding this: "We have not even to risk the adventure alone, for the heroes of all times have gone before us, the labyrinth is thoroughly known. We have only to follow the thread of the hero path and where we had thought to slay another, we should slay ourselves, and where we had thought to travel outward we shall come to the center of our own existence and where we had thought to be alone we shall be with all the world" (Joseph Campbell with Bill Moyers *Power of Myth:* 1988).

At one of our earliest Life Long Directions Personal and Spiritual Growth Workshops, we asked each participant to bring to the final session a line of poetry or prose or a scripture passage that best described where he/she was in his/her life at that time. One man fussed all week not knowing how to find something that reflected himself at that moment. Sharing this with his wife, she immediately responded, "I know the perfect line for you. It is from the story of the marriage feast of Cana in the Gospel of John: 'What you have done is kept the choice wine until last (John 2:10b).' " The Greater Self has been involved in engineering the ego development of life's first half, perhaps unbeknown to you. But this is the time the Self has been waiting for, the marriage feast, "the best is yet to be," "the choice wine last."

However, these ideas are counterculture. The culture acclaims youth, not age. Yet, in so doing, youth is greatly diminished when its only anticipation is inevitable mortal decline; deterioration and death. How much more wonderful for youth to know that all the stages of life are for new growth, creativity, the becoming of the Self, and for Soul making. This is the invitation that follows youth.

> Grow old along with me!
> The best is yet to be,
> The last of life for which the first was made.

As Jung said, not only are midlife and old age not just a "sorry append-age" to youth, but they are the reason for childhood and youth. Birth, childhood, and youth exist for the purpose of the Soul making that goes on in life's second half. We are each invited to conscious aging. Aging consciously calls for, not simply gathering chronological years, but engaging in a psychological and spiritual movement within one's total being, Soul making.

Our greater Self tells us that these precious years, these days of our lives, these times of long life are in the hands of God. Each of us is in the hands of the Creator. The popular Broadway musical, *Into the Woods,* (Stephen Sondheim) gives us the refrain to chant, "You are not alone, no one is alone." Each of us is accompanied by the greater Self, by God and by those who have walked before us. The image of God within, tells us, *"you are not alone."* Browning, true to his historical moment, uses the masculine pronoun in referring to God, *"his* hands." Your greater Self, your inner Poet may also wisely say, "You are in *her* hands." As we were each created in the sublime vessel of a woman's body, this can be an appropriate image for the new creation going on in the aging process, and for the God who fashions us.

> Our times are in his (her) hands
> Who saith, "A whole I planned;
> Youth shows but half. Trust God; see all, nor be afraid."

This is an invitation to full participation in the second half of life. The Self invites us to embark upon this growth in consciousness, "see all," that only long life can provide. We are called to enter into the spirit journey that each new decade gives. We are challenged to accept lovingly and passionately the Soul making innate in the aging process. "See all, nor be afraid." Be not afraid of the shadow manifestations that come as they call you to great heights.

When a person climbs a mountain and reaches the top, he or she looks down and has a total and more complete breathtaking view. Long life is an invitation to the manifestations of life lived to completion, as a part of the whole life of creation itself, as part of the Spirit Life of God's own great Soul. Midlife and old age are simply life's process of refining and regenerating a Soul. And how much our world needs great Souls making their mark upon our cultures. Today each of us given the gift of long life is invited to be an explorer of all of midlife's peaks and finally the summit of a vital old age. At the same time, we are called to be archaeologists of our own neglected inner world that gives each of us both depth and meaning.

Growing in All Four Stages of Life

Growing into the World

We began this book with many portraits of people in later midlife and in the mature years who have continued to grow. There are many who would scoff at the idea of growth in what looks for all the world like unmitigated decline. In this chapter, we want to look more closely at human growth—especially human psychological and spiritual growth in all the stages of life. To see it in more depth may help us to discern breathtaking growth where before we could observe only the facade of diminishment.

We take for granted the growth in life's first half. The physical development is so obvious. Birth announcements include the size of the newborn. Year by year the measuring tape and scale record the physical signs of the enormous development of an infant into a baby—into a toddler—into a child, adolescent, young adult, adult. We expect the physical growth, but just as truly, we expect the growth in consciousness, the emotional growth, relational growth, intellectual growth, the growth in skills. We are disappointed when they fail to happen on schedule. We know that the babbling of the infant will turn into vowel sounds, into that thunderous first word, into the nonstop verbosity of the teen. From the frustrating struggle to turn over at five months, to the running away of the two-year-old, to the walk down the aisle of the young adult, as awesome as each moment is, it is expected. It is nurtured, cherished, promoted, and paid for by the whole culture around the young person.

Our young are prodded and pushed, taught and retaught how to grow up and be a grown up. There are milestones that measure success, programs that are built into the family's and society's demands that its young become able, able-bodied, educated, socialized contributors to society.

The individuality is there and nourished to a degree but there are always universal, uniform expectations of the two or the twelve- and twenty-year-old. There are these ladders to climb. One moves from grade one to grade two to three toward graduation, job, marriage or not, military service or not, promotion or not, parenthood or not, job mobility or not, home ownership or not.

"There was something of a conveyor belt for the first half of my life," a doctor said recently. "After college and premed, I went on to medical school. Then, I had to do my internship and spend time overseas in the service. Then, there followed my marriage, the apartment, residency in my specialization, my first practice as a partner, my own practice, the house and the three kids. I'm forty-nine now the kids are raised, the practice is OK, and the conveyor belt is stalled. What now? Where do I go from here?"

"There was a script and the script stopped here," said a midlife woman. Another woman, a fifty-year-old said, "I was a daughter, and now my parents are dead. I was a wife and now I'm divorced. I was a mother and now the kids are raised and live all over the country. I was a teacher and I took early retirement, so who am I now?"

They are all talking about the world into which each of us is born, a particular society and its accepted expectations and roles. Whether we measure up or not, get to the top of the ladder or not, there seem to be certain goals to which we are expected to measure up. There seems to be a kind of consensus out there, certain standards by which we can measure our own growth and development. Early in life, they give us direction. Without them, we might not have survived. If someone did not make traffic laws, and someone did not say, "Don't you dare put your foot in that gutter," we would not have made it to three. If we did not learn a language in its particular local accent or did not go to school, so much of ourselves would have remained dormant and undeveloped. In the hands of truly loving people who care about us, and want us to develop our own unique gifts as well as to mature into healthy, productive members of this world, the people around us and the culture make enormous contributions to the growth of each of us.

At the wedding of two recently graduated young medical interns a few years ago, one could see that early outside world of these two young adults well represented by the loving people who had raised them and nurtured them. There, at their wedding reception, was the childhood and early adulthood of these two *twenty-something* doctors. Sitting at round tables were the representatives of their outside world to the present. The guest list had been carefully divided into compatible groups at the different tables. Each table's guests represented the different places, times, and parts of the couple's lives. This was their outside environment. These were the people who were very responsible for their growth until now, responsible for whom they had become thus far. There were the two tables of parents; hers Irish, German; his Korean. Here was his early world, born in Korea, moved to New York; hers, born in New York, moved to New Jersey. There were tables of the siblings that filled those early homes and were now all in the wedding party—his brother; her three brothers and two sisters with their spouses. There were six tables of aunts and uncles and cousins on both sides. They were all remembering them through all their early stages and telling stories of parties and games and mishaps of the years of their lives. There were many stories about vacations spent together in the same resorts and about the feats of daring of the bride from her earliest days. Then, there were the tables of friends, teachers, coaches, college professors, bosses. There were tables of friends of their parents from each different stage of their lives, and their own childhood friends, college friends, and two tables of friends from the last five years of their lives at medical school and in internship.

The bride and groom, visiting these last two tables of young doctors, were immersed in the tales of the new world that was presently so important to them, as to be almost all-consuming. That medical world had its own language and mores, issues that were largely mysterious to the rest of the guests. Yet no one present had any doubt that the world of medicine and these other doctors were the most significant influence on the personality development of these two young doctors now, just as each of the other groups had been at earlier stages of development. Even their meeting and choice of one another as life partner had been in and through this medical environment. No one had any doubt that the medical profession they had chosen would dictate much of who they would be and become in the next several years.

So it is with all the choices and relationships of young adulthood. Each of us takes on the mores of the business and groups we enter. The great difference between youth and childhood is that in childhood we have little or no choice of what the outside world that influences us will be. We do not choose our parents, or our family. In young adulthood, on the other hand, we choose our new environments. Then, they take over from the influence of parents, early family, friends, and all the parent substitutes to become the primary influence on our growth and development. The people, events and culture of those childhood and young adulthood years are the great sources of our personality and character development. In this first half of life the outside environment is the primary influence on our growth and development. It is primarily through and in these influences that our ego is formed or malformed. That is the first half of life, the first thirty-five, forty or forty-five or so years. Then, this outside world steps far back, its work done, for better or worse. At this point, for most, ego consciousness is securely there. We know who we are. At least, we have a pretty good idea what we like and do not like, stand for or do not stand for; what we shall do or shall not do; to whom we relate or do not relate. We know so much about ourselves and our view of the world that if we were to try to write it down, it would stretch across a country.

Carl Jung said that in the first half of life, the primary influence on our growth and development comes from the outside environment. If then, we make the transition into the second half of life—and not everyone who lives to be forty, fifty, sixty, does make this psychological transition; there are eighty-year-olds who have never made a midlife transition—if we make this psychological transition, then the outside environment is *no longer the primary influence* on our growth and development. The primary influence on the personality and character growth and development in life's second half comes from *within* the individual. The primary influence now comes from our own psyche, our own soul, our own inner depths with all the potentials of those inner depths. Growth comes now from our own untapped, dormant, unknown self. It comes from our unconscious self. In Carl Jung's personality theory this unconscious Self is a womb of new growth, a source of untold potential. More seasoned in life now, we can step beyond—and look back to see the people, the events, the culture; see the times, class, gender, and family expectations that circumscribed our earlier consciousness. Our blinders, as it were, start to fall off. Jung calls this the process of Individuation; the becoming of one's true Self.

Just when I think I am all grown up and have it pretty much together; just when I finally know myself pretty well, just when everyone around me thinks they know me well, the ground shifts beneath me.

There is always so much more to me than I know. I started life totally unconscious, unaware. Then my ego developed simultaneously as I grew in consciousness. I became more and more aware. People around me worked very hard to help me become more and more aware. Yet now, as I cross the threshold into life's second half, the floodgates can open. What lay dormant, unconscious within erupts, gradually or suddenly. A new me begins to see the light. "I don't know what's gotten into me," I say. "I don't know what's gotten into you," they say. What was within untapped, seduces, demands its day, its time. I am ready now to become more and more my own true self. When the time is ripe, the greater Self unseats my ego and takes the lead. I am ready now to move beyond the collective "scripts" and "conveyer belts." I begin to ask questions I never asked before, think thoughts I never thought before, want what I never wanted before, say what I never said before, do what I never did before.

The psychic energy, until now given over to the work of making a niche for myself in the outside world; the energy that went into adapting to my worlds and building my empire, seems suddenly to be withdrawn from all that. The energy that went into climbing the ladder and taking care of business, and the business of getting through the day, and taking care of others seems missing somehow.

Growing throughout the Whole
Second Half of Life

Jung tells us that great psychic energy is being given over to my unconscious self, what he calls my number two personality, which is being readied to emerge. When this begins to happen, perhaps it feels like the wind is taken out of my sails. I can begin to feel apathy, lethargy, boredom, ennui, a sense of: "It's the same old thing, I can barely get myself up and out." I feel the monotony of my life. I am depressed, have no enthusiasm for what once was so important; indeed for what was important only yesterday. This feels like the burnouts of burnouts. One woman said, "I feel becalmed, like the wind is gone out of my sails." "This marriage, or at least me in this marriage, feels stalled," said another woman. "I feel stopped in my tracks, I have no energy for anything," said a high-powered male executive. The energy, the vitality has moved away from what were the meanings, values, and goals that got us to where we are, so that new parts of my personality, dormant until now, may begin to operate. Perhaps, it will be the poet, or the teacher or the author or a thousand other possibilities that will begin to emerge. This time of feeling overwhelming deadness can indeed be a time of profound growth, as new parts of myself are readied, begin to stir within me and yet, the whole thing feels like death, disgust, and disillusionment with my life.

I (Anne) remember when I first began to feel these kinds of feelings in my early forties. I remember being filled with enthusiasm for a cause. I had become aware of a great injustice in the area where I lived and worked and I, along with several others, was determined to do something about this evil situation. I could think and talk of little else during the spring and a good part of the summer of that year. One man in our group had been elected to a small community office and he was to chair our group. I spent some time away studying and on vacation during the summer. I met him at a social event shortly after my return, and he asked me what night I would be free during the next week. "I know how important this issue is to you, and I want to be sure to select a night when you're free," he said. I felt my stomach sink. I felt that I did not want to go to that meeting or any meeting. I felt totally disinterested in the whole thing. I put on a good front and dragged myself to the meetings but my heart was not in it. This was not typical of me. I was not the kind of person who gets the ball rolling and then moves on to a new thing and gets another ball rolling. I have always tended to stay with things and finish what I start. "What's the matter with me?" I thought. Then it began to happen in all the other areas of my life. I carried on my life as usual. I would be working with people on a project or even preparing a prayer service or attending a prayer service, and I felt like a spectator. My heart was not in it. I had an enormous faith crisis, far greater than ever before.

I had an enormous crisis of meaning. What a waste my life had been, I thought. What a fool to ignore the possibility of marriage and children! What a waste of my life to choose to be a nun. I remember writing in my journal that year, "I feel like my life has been canceled." "Acedia," it was once called, losing one's place in the universe, in the scheme of things. I had not only lost enthusiasm for my life, I was filled with angst, anger, and regret about my choices. As I lived with that pain for more than two years, it began to call me to make some big changes in my life.

When I read that journal entry about my life being canceled these many years later, I think that my life was not canceled, but I was closed for repairs. I was closed for major alterations. This was what is called a liminal, an in-between time. All of the things I have done and become since, getting a doctorate, writing several books, cofounding, codirecting Mid-Life Directions, being an international facilitator, fighting a battle against ageism, and most of all, having a deeper prayer life and a stronger faith life than ever (because it was able to incorporate doubt) would have been unimaginable to the person I was back then. It is not that I never feel the loss of the things I might have had, those feelings come and go. It is that a deeper part of me has taken the lead. I am again and again recommitting. I have a sense that I am where I am supposed to be and it will be from here that I will grow even more into my Self, God's dream for me.

It could have gone the other way, I could have moved beyond my initial commitment, made a new and different life choice. For many, this is the right way to go—the way the greater Self, the soul is leading, and so God's dream for that person. In any case, growth would have happened, if the person holds on to the basic core of self that the early choices reflect. Yet, it is also possible to be untrue to oneself, to "throw the baby out with the bathwater." This would be regression, not growth.

It is also just as possible to refuse growth by ignoring or drowning these new feelings and questionings, taking a stiff upper lip approach to these inner movements of the midlife crisis of feelings, and then, just dig in and stagnate. This is obviously not growth either, it is dying at forty or fifty and not getting buried until eighty or ninety.

People in these initial stages of the midlife transition often say, about one or other parts of their lives and relationships, "My heart isn't in it anymore." That's an amazing phrase, *my heart isn't in it*. As new and unconscious parts of ourselves begin to emerge, new and unrecognized aspects of us take our heart, our energy, our passion.

We can begin to feel hatred and resentment for these choices of our earlier life. The new passion can emerge not only in fatal attractions but in anger about every choice I've made. I can begin to hate what I have loved and love what I have hated.

People in this midlife crisis of negative feelings scream: "What a fool I've been giving everything to this marriage (to this company . . . to this profession . . . to this institution)!"

"What did I ever see in him . . . in her!?"

"I've given everything to this corporation who knows? Who cares? They could just flick me away like a piece of dust."

"I never really loved you, I married you because I got you pregnant (or you got me pregnant)."

"I married you because you were a great dancer. Some good that has done me in the last twenty years!"

"I became a lawyer only because my father wanted it."

"For a year," one woman said, "I said every day, I think I hate him. Then, for another year I said, maybe I don't hate him but I sure don't like him. Then, for another nine months it was, well, maybe he's not so bad. Finally, it got to, maybe I really do love him. I know that the *I love him* of today is from someplace deep within me, and that the person I love is a new and gentler man. Because while I was going through my hate phase, I know he had his."

Not every midlife couple waits out the feelings until they shift. For some, of course, the awakening is to the *fact,* not just the feeling that there never really has been a marriage.

For some there is a call to a new career, profession, geography, or lifestyle. For some the call will be to a change of the way of doing or being the same thing; or perhaps staying in the same but somehow different marriage.

The midlife *crisis of feelings* which we have been discussing, and the midlife crisis are not exactly the same thing. The midlife crisis itself is a developmental crisis, like the birth crisis or the adolescent crisis. That means it is about whether a person will or will not move on. The birth crisis means it is time to move on from the once comfortable environment of the womb. The time for the birth is the beginning of the birth crisis. Because all the growing and developing that can go on in the womb has gone on, for this tiny person to go on growing and developing, he or she must get out and move on. This is archetypal, that is, it is built into the growth process of every human person.

Now, at midlife, something similar is happening. All the growing and developing that can come about primarily through the influence of the outside world has happened, it is time for a new kind of growth. The invitation is archetypal. It is built in. For most of us, though not all, the invitation comes through what we have come to call *a crisis of negative feelings.* So many people whom we have met in these years of conducting Mid-Life Directions Workshops for Personal and Spiritual Growth, are in the midst of these awful feelings of apathy, boredom, lethargy, or they are caught into disillusionment, anxiety, anger and regret, that we have come to believe that most people go through a crisis of negative feelings at the beginning of the midlife transition. There are, of course, smooth evolvers, who seem to grow through the midlife transition rather easily, but they seem to be out-numbered by the others. At every workshop that we conduct one or more people tell us something like, "Thank God, I'm not losing my mind, what I'm feeling is normal." This initiation into mid-life is a dying and a new birth, and for most there are some labor pains.

Unfortunately, there are some people who get caught into these negative feelings and never move beyond the lethargy, or cynicism, the anger and regret. There are many bitter, angry old people who spend their years in moroseness, despair, or fury at themselves and those whom they blame for their early choices.

There is a saying that midlife is getting to the top of the ladder and finding the ladder is against the wrong roof. One needs to stay with these feelings and not jump too quickly to a new roof. Eventually, the feelings of anger and regret may fuel the development to which the Self is leading one. The feelings will cause us to pause and take a closer, more objective, and deeper look at who it is who has been climbing the ladder.

As my ego begins to take a back seat, and my greater Self takes the *lead,* I am certain that I know where it is at when I'm forty but then, by fifty, I'm so much wiser and know that I really do not know anything.

We remember a woman who seemed to be quite sure of everything in her forties. When we first met her she had yet to experience any of the movements of the midlife transition. She came to a Mid-Life Directions

Workshop and on the first evening, leaving her husband in the back of the meeting room to talk with some friends, she came to us in the front. "I don't know if we made a mistake in coming here," she blurted out. "I said to my husband, on the way here, 'I don't know what we're going to get out of this weekend. After all our life together has been so great that anything good that happens to us after this is going to be icing on the cake.' "

She was forty-three. While this seems like a positive statement, it manifested very low expectations for a life that could last thirty, forty, or fifty more years. That surely would be a lot of "icing." She was saying that all the real living was over. All the real stuff had been done.

Indeed, some very real living had gone on. She was a charming, well liked, well educated person. They had worked hard and succeeded at their marriage. They had done a great job in their parenting. They now had three sons doing well in college. They were affluent. He had been very successful in his career and she had supported him and made great contributions all along the way. She had been a creative homemaker and had chosen to be a full time homemaker and mother. She had a very real faith life and had been active in both her community and church. Now, she has no consciousness yet, of the changes in store for her and of the enormous potential dormant within her. She has yet to confront the losses and glories ahead. Yet, we had some hints that she would probably soon be on her way. First, she had come to a midlife workshop. What made her come at all? Then, she was so extremely anxious that we (and she) know how great everything was for them that she had to blurt it out immediately.

When we encountered the same woman some years later in a follow-up workshop, she was well into her fifties. Their three sons had married, one was divorced and raising two children on his own. She and her husband were very involved. She had "three other incredible grandchildren." Her husband had had bypass surgery and gone to a very serious rehab program. He had made some profound lifestyle changes. He was on a strict low fat diet and meditated twice a day. He had stayed with the same company and things on the surface looked quite the same for this vice president of his corporation. Yet, she told us he was so different, had grown less aggressive and was "much easier to live with." He was very into the grandparenting and loved his days building with Habitat for Humanity.

She had had a "major upheaval" a year after the midlife workshop. "The bottom dropped out. I became involved with this wonderful man I had met. The affair lasted only a short time, but I had begun to feel so trapped in my life, so sick to death of everything I was involved in. I decided, after eleven months of this sick feeling in the pit of my stomach to take a few classes. I think it was just to do something different." She went on to tell us that she got hooked, went back to school, got the BA she had almost finished before her marriage. She went on to get two other degrees and now had her own counseling practice.

When we reminded her of her "icing on the cake" remark, she said that she did not remember it. Then she told us, "That was another woman you met back there, our marriage now is a different marriage and indeed today our life together is not bad at all. The paradox is I almost lost him and the marriage to really learn what I thought I knew then. Now, I know I don't know much at all and I keep waiting for the next surprises."

Aniella Jaffe, an analyst who was once Jung's secretary said that in the second half of life you cannot understand the world if you do not understand paradox. As consciousness expands and expands exponentially, we see how mysterious life and everything else really are. We trace our finger over the outline of our limitations as we grow more conscious. We say good-bye to the beautiful naiveté of youth when we believed ourselves to be infinite and eternal. Now that I know more and have become more aware, I kiss disillusionment. The illusions of youth slip away.

In the second half of life, we have seen the face of death. We have begun to come in contact with our own mortality. The face in the mirror is no longer young. We begin to experience the losses and diminishments of aging. Health becomes an even bigger issue. We may even find it entering too often into conversations with friends and family. We may be diagnosed as suffering a chronic condition like high blood pressure or slowed thyroid. The ravages of time seem to be overtaking us. Our skin, glands, metabolism begin to suffer battle fatigue. We look in the mirror and cannot believe it. The wrinkles and loose skin, the hair loss, perhaps, reading glasses for the first time, or all the symptoms leading to menopause shock us.

We may experience new sexual problems, waning desire, impotence, or frigidity, boredom and loss of interest. On the other hand, we may have a new sexual awakening, a feeling of being oversexed and too often aroused by too many people. We may find ourselves attracted to someone very much younger than ourselves over and over again. One man told us that he had a series of affairs with his daughters' peer group until he realized that he was really on a quest for the youth in himself and even more in need of the undeveloped feminine side of himself.

Death becomes much more real. We are very deeply touched by the loss of a peer. Over and over throughout the second half of life we go to the funerals, one after the other, of the whole older generation of our family and we look around for those who used to be in charge, only to find that it is our generation that is in charge now. Then, we are even more shocked as our siblings, and cousins in our generation start to go. The loss of a parent is always a profound human experience, whenever it happens in a person's life. For most, it happens in midlife or sometime in the second half of life. When our parents die, it feels as if something that we have been standing on has given way. It is as though a black hole has swallowed up something beneath us. No matter how supportive or nonsupportive our parents have been, they have always been there. Now they are not. If they have been a great, and wonderful presence in our lives, their loss is a terrible emotional wrenching. In any case, their deaths put us face to face with our own mortality. It seems as if they have stood between us and our own death and now, they are gone.

In a culture that worships youth, people in the second half of life can very early on begin to feel obsolete. The faces and bodies in the magazines are the young ones in a society whose beauty standard is a *twenty-something* one. One *forty-something* woman said, "I remembered how I ran to the restroom to hide my tears at my first college mother/son social. We were on the dance floor when my son said to me, 'I've never been in a room with so many old hags in my life.'" We can begin to run from exercise club to exercise club, from plastic surgeon to plastic surgeon in a never-ending quest to recapture our lost youth. Others of us realize eventually that it is time to discard the cultural and societal stereotypes and to begin our contribution to changing the standard of beauty with or without some help from technology.

People begin to feel edged out in the places where they work as younger men and women come into the workplace with so many experiences that were not possible in an earlier time. We see that they may have a breath of experiences but they do not have the depth of experience that comes from living life. As we move through the second half of life, we can feel more and more victims of *ageist* attitudes. Perhaps we are downsized while less dedicated and more inexperienced people with less sound judgment are not. All this takes a great deal of grieving. Yet, all this can cause us to change our focus from a myopic concentration of livelihood to a focus on *life*. We come to know that our livelihood is not our life. We come to know that our work is a part of life but not the whole of it.

As we move through the seven to ten or so years of the midlife transition and well into the second half of life, we have seen the faces of death, loss, and diminishment. We have come to know that while youth may have been a gift of nature, age is a work of art. We have tasted our power to prevail, survive, overcome and even blossom. As Christopher Fry says in *A Sleep of the Prisoners*, this is the time for the longest stride of our souls:

> Affairs are now soul size
> The enterprise
> Is exploration onto God

This is the sphere of human evolution in our times. Not only is this the time when we are beginning to move into the realization of full humanity for women as well as men, it is the time of the doubling of the life cycle. The sphere of evolution is the biological, psychological, spiritual gift of a second lifetime. At the beginning of this third millennium, we have been given a double lifespan. "A girl child born now," said a recent headline, "can expect to live to be 103 and a boy slightly less." The eighty-five-year-olds are the fastest growing population in the United States. The population in the second half of life is no longer a minority population. It is absolutely crucial to the survival of the human race that the members of this new population explosion each become all they can become. It is crucial that this large population in the second half of life be recognized as the gift to the human race that it is. Yet, the aging population is talked about and dealt with, not as a gift, but as a problem and a drain. People in the second half of life are talked about by the political and so called *real* world in terms of needs only. In her book, *The Fountain of Age*, Betty Friedan says: "We are not the problem, we are the solution."

Wisdom and age are a solution. We desperately need people who have become experienced in the process of aging. We need people who are continuing to grow and to become all they can be, all through their lives. This book is about that urgent need for each person who is chronologically in the second half of life to move psychologically and spiritually into the second half of life. It is also a plea to each of us who is aging to be a splendid and striking witness to the wealth and hidden power of a long life.

Yet, everyone knows that it is possible to die at forty-five or fifty and not get buried until eighty. It's possible to die at sixty or seventy and not get buried until ninety. It is *these living dead* who give us the populist picture of midlife and old age. It's these *dead* who give later midlife and the mature years a bad name. Too many people who reach the turning point of the midlife crisis, which like the birth crisis is a jolting invitation to move on and to move out, just flip out or get stuck.

Many people go into a severe regression when confronted with the signs of aging. They throw everything over. They abandon roles, responsibilities, relationships, commitments, character when confronted by the first whispers from the unconscious. The first glimpse of awareness that something I once valued and chose is really not so great anymore after all, or perhaps *never was* great for me, sends them into reverse gear. These first murmurs from the other side of the personality become the invitation to panic and run amok and/or become completely cynical about half a lifetime. They get misinterpreted as the need to throw everything over and to go around again, one more time. So, someone changes the places, the people, the commitments, and substitutes others, *not* from deep within the Self but merely in imitation of the current youth culture. All this movement looks different, can even pass for change, be mistaken for growth. However, it is just resurfacing. Such a person is still living up to the expectations of the *outside environment,* still being named and moved by society. Now it is the present youth culture's mores and values. A person who regresses into a series of affairs or into a cocoon of drugs and alcohol is missing the messages from the Self, from the Soul. A person who gets caught in a frenetic existence of materialism, or social activity, or workaholism, or golfaholism, or even unremitting evangelism or social action is not growing from within. Perhaps such persons have not even acknowledged the existence of a within. Perhaps such persons have yet to recognize their own uniqueness, their own souls. They eventually probably burn out and go out with a whimper. In the later years they may regress all the way to become childish, helpless burdens to everyone around them.

This counterfeit midlife crisis is really better called midlife craziness. Unfortunately, there are so many stories of people who take this route that most of us have met them and can tell stories of our own. Speaking to an adult son and daughter of such a man, once a "model" husband and father, they told us that their father left when he turned fifty. He started a series of affairs with very young women. "He's not married to the one he lives with now, and is always trying to impress us with how cool and 'with it' he is. Talking to him is like talking to a kid younger than we are."

We all regress a bit to pick up parts of ourselves that need to be lived in some way but here we are not referring to this, but to what Jung calls an overthrow of the ego, a swing to the other side. It is important to see that there is a world of difference between these kinds of regressions and people who keep the child and youth alive within themselves. We all need an ongoing relationship with the Child within ourselves. We need to let him or her out frequently. It is the Child in us who will be curious and energize us to try the new. It is the Child who will lead us to *newness* of life since the Child *is* new life. It is the Child in us who will be able to take us through the last great death and the last great birth of our lives. Jesus knew the psychological and spiritual difference when he said, "Unless you become like a little child, you shall not enter the kingdom." It is significant that he said *like* a child and not unless you become a child.

There are other people in the second half of life who do not regress but do not move on either. They just get stuck. They decay, decline. They are rigid. They turn into pillars of salt. They look back, look back to the good old days. They have answered all life's questions. They do not allow doubt or questioning of any belief, choice or value to come to the surface. They are certain that they know all the answers. They know what they should do about everything and what everyone else *should* do. Dogmatic, closed, one-sided, they fear uncertainty and ambiguity. They cannot really abide mystery. They have made their gods idols and they have made their stagnant values gods.

Vast areas of living remain totally beyond their ken. They remain unconscious of vast areas of life. For them, moments of darkness and uncertainty are not invitations to explore and trust, they are times for the wet blankets of dogmas and clichés. People who are stuck are one-sided, prejudiced, judgmental, critical, carping, complaining. They say again and again, to themselves, and to others, "I never did that before and I'm certainly not going to start now." Over and over they say and live, "It's too late."

Some stuck people, mask the genuine anxiety innate to this time of failing body, and confrontation with mortality by holding to unswerving routines and rituals. They can become violent with anyone who disrupts their routine even for a dire emergency. A young mother who lived in a different state from her mother told us that when she called to ask to bring her new baby to see his grandmother for the first time, she was too busy to see them. Mother made her wait until her next trip home to introduce her new grandchild because this was the day for her washing and ironing. Even the introduction of a new grandchild was not enough reason to change this woman's routine.

People who get stuck remain egocentric just as people who regress remain egocentric. Each decade of stuckness or regression grows more ugly. Each decade makes it more impossible to hold back the inundation of the unconscious aspects of the self that have not been accepted, received, and integrated. Each decade makes it more difficult to recognize the potentials for growth that come before such a person.

All the stories we told in chapter 1, and many of the others we are yet to tell, are stories of real people who have neither regressed nor gotten stuck. There is a wonderful woman whose story we have told many times, because she is such a great example of the fullness of life, and continuing growth and development until the end of life. She lived well into her nineties, always open, growing, changing, becoming. She suffered many of the physical losses of the aging process, including losing most of her sight. She did many of the things unsighted people do to compensate for her loss, including trying to learn to read Braille. Like her, we all have a great deal we can learn from people with handicaps who have been able to build their handicap into their image of themselves without totally identifying themselves with their handicap. Such people are able to say, "I have this disability, but I am far more than this disability."

This woman was a wisdom figure for younger people around her. She would truly listen to them because she was never in competition with the young. She asked challenging questions out of her years of experience. She had moved from one career to the other through the whole second half of her life. Now she was retired many years. As she grew smaller in frame, she grew bigger in her expansive mind and heart and spirit. She would be the one to whom people around her would come when they wanted to try out on someone who was wise some new ideas about a new enterprise they were contemplating. She would ask questions out of her vast experience, make suggestions and always affirm. People never felt put down by her. When asked once what was the secret of such a vital life at her age, she said only, "Never get stuck. There are people around who had a heart attack at fifty and got stuck in it."

Unfortunately, we have all met people who have gotten stuck, I have had the temptation many times myself. The temptations to regress or to get stuck are great. The trials, losses, and challenges of aging are enormous. Yet, the stakes are even greater. They are each person's precious life, irreplaceable personality and humanity's ongoing growth and evolution as well.

So much growth in the second half of life is growth in consciousness. I integrate into my personality, into my life what I was once totally unconscious of. Individuation is the process of little by little becoming more whole, more and more my Self. This goes on as I meet life head on and live out the new parts of myself as they are called forth by my life experiences and as they emerge from my depths. There is no point in life where I can abandon myself or give up on myself. There is no time when I am finished, or when God is finished creating me. If eternal life means anything, it means that too. Creation is ongoing through all the stages and ages of life. I am not only God's work of art, I am sharing in the infinite creativity. If God is infinite, God's dream for me is infinite. My death is my last great birth. Here as in a mirror, darkly, I image God. Then, face to face, I will flower and flourish, a revelation of God for all eternity. Life in all of its stages is a glorious adventure.

In an interview for the BBC, Carl Jung, at eighty-one, said that he had treated many old people. He observed that in aging adults their unconscious side ignores the fact that they are apparently threatened with the complete end. "We are not sure that it is a complete end," he said, "because Life behaves as if it is going on. So I tell old people to live on, as if they had centuries, and then, they will live properly."

Certainly, one needs to make realistic concessions to the aging process. Yet, the slowing down of the body is for deepening, not for vegetating and inertia. There is so much teeming life within each of us that needs to unfold in this world. There is so much each of us can give back to the environment that had such a big part in bringing us to the second half of life and will never cease playing some part in our growing.

Four Women: Four Stages

There is an image indelibly impressed on my (Anne) psyche. It is an image of the four stages of life. It is an image of four women, four generations, each involved in dying and being born.

It was a March day. The earth asleep for a long snowy winter was the promise of very early spring. There was new life in the cold. The oldest of the four women, Ann, would die on June 21, the spring equinox, the first day of summer of that year. She was eighty-eight. She was very ill. No one knew quite how ill, but still moving around her little house. Her midlife daughter, Eileen—in her forties—had come to see her and brought with her the greatest gift that she had yet given her. Eileen had brought her daughter, Noreen, just days before transformed into a mother, at 26, and with her the old woman's new great granddaughter. Meghan was just a few weeks old.

It was a comfortable everyday scene. The white-haired great grandmother was in a warm light gray jogging suit; no one else was dressed up. The oldest woman was in *her* corner on her couch, a red quilt under her and her short legs up. The dark-haired new mother sat on the edge of the couch near her grandmother's knees and put down the tiny baby girl, while holding her still in a sitting-up position, on her grandmother's lap. The baby's face was looking into the old woman's face. Those new eyes looked fixedly into those old bright Irish eyes. I still see the look that transfixed them and those graceful alabaster hands, which had diapered seven babies of her own, playing with the tiny baby fingers. The young woman, still sore from the emergency C section, that had invalidated all their Lamaze classes, was looking intently at her grandmother for a response to her firstborn. The expectancy and awe, the questioning smile, asking from the core of her newly fruitful womanhood, said only: "What do you think, Grandma, this is Meghan!" Anne's face shone, a mirror for the new life in her arms. She smiled a wonderful smile at the baby and through the infant right through to the young girl mother who had once been a baby on those same knees. Then, she looked at her daughter, Eileen, baby of her seven children, the new grandmother who had tears in her eyes. The look they exchanged was an all-knowing look. This mother and daughter were sharing an experience beyond speech. That look plummeted each woman into the core of the mystery of life. These women together were in God, the feminine face and revelation of God. I knew that I was in a sanctuary.

No one said much, no one could. This moment was a hole in time and space, all contemplative. The looking was drawing in an explosion of emotion and meaning. The words that were said were addressed to the baby, "See, Meggie. See, this is your great grandmother." The words were addressed to the one who could see and understand the least. She was the most unconscious of the four, but the one who at some level of her tiny being that day absorbed a Love beyond understanding. The one who could see the most, even though her eyes were dim was seeing what can be seen and known, only by someone who has lived a long life, and generated a daughter, a granddaughter, and a great granddaughter. The mystery of such a knowing has been revealed to only a special few until now. Living great grandmothers or great grandfathers have never before in human history been so plentiful.

Meghan had grown for nine months in her mother's womb. She was nourished and housed in a warm security with all her needs being met. Mother and fetus had been surrounded by a young husband/father's protective love. When all the growing and developing that could go on there had been accomplished, the only way for her to go on growing and developing was to get out, to move on. She had to die to that way of growing and being nourished. She had to die to the womb in order to be born a child. She would spend her next years in a new womb, the womb of childhood, psychically wedded to her parents, the environments, and the culture they gave her.

In adolescence, there would be crisis. She would die again, now to childhood, to be born a youth. Her twenty-six-year-old mother had recently gone through her own adolescent transition into young adulthood. Her marriage, and the birth of Meghan had been the end of that transition into young adulthood for Noreen. Looking back, I can see how definitive a step into adulthood this process of becoming a mother was in the long process of Noreen's adolescent death to childhood and birth into adulthood. So obvious was this her metamorphosis, and the move that placed her among the adults of the family, that her younger brother and her cousins started to tease her by calling her "Aunt Noreen" in the year after Meghan's birth.

Eileen too, the new grandmother in her forties, was in her midlife crisis/transition. Her younger, "Happy-go-lucky" self had recently given way to someone with greater depth and a new, and more nuanced version of the caring self, that had always been her way. Yet, that dying to be born anew had been a terribly painful struggle for Eileen, as she had coped with the end of the kind of mothering that had been so core to her own first half of life. Even her job choices and immersion in her community had a lot to do with being there for her family. Now she was free to move in her own directions, but the shape of that direction had yet to emerge. Looking back now, the road she eventually chose has not been to live through her grandchildren. She has begun a new career and begun to develop whole new parts of herself. Of course, she still manages to be a grandmother who is experiencing life through the eyes of her grandchildren and thoroughly enjoying it and them.

Ann too was in the process of dying that day. She was not going easily. She did not want to die. In a brush with death two years before, she had said, "If God wants me, God will have to come and get me, I'm not going!" She feared death with a terrible dread even though she still clung desperately to hope for new life beyond the grave. In that last year however, she had a dream that fought for space in her psyche and emotions. It was a hope-filled dream. In the dream, she saw a priest who told her to go to the top of the hill. There at the top of the hill she saw her husband. (She was a widow for twelve years.) He was very happy and with great love he invited her to sit down with him at a square table.

Ann, a matter-of-fact, unemotional person, was not much into dreams. Yet, this one had a very powerful emotional impact on her. Its power was reinforced by a synchronistic event. The priest in the dream was someone who had visited her often in her illness. She told him that he had been in her dream and then told him the dream. Amazed, he told her that at the time she had the dream he was in Europe on a pilgrimage, and that indeed, he had directed his group to the top of the hill where he had celebrated Mass for them on a square altar. The pilgrimage was to a Mary Shrine. Both Mary, the mother of Jesus, and the Mass were of supreme importance to Ann. When she was told that a square is often the symbol of wholeness and completion, she had a great sense of the importance of her dream.

In the last year, often in great pain, she would say over and over again like a mantra, "the top of the hill . . . the top of the hill." At her funeral, the Mass of the Resurrection, the story of that dream was printed on the inside cover of the program. As part of the eulogy, her oldest son told the story of the dream. At the end, in a loud, if slightly shaking voice, he proclaimed to her, and to a full church, "You are at the top of the hill now, Ann."

Spirit Receiving: Spirit Giving

THE ROSE

by Anne Brennan

All green, tight, closed tiny promise of
All that will unfold in swelling.
Grace; gift who calls you out.
I wait by your promise playing in the dirt
At the roots.
Letting go one programmed morning in the much too cold
You test birth from your safety, one petal at a time.
Bending back upside down, letting ripe red only show.
A slit of fire, reaching out, seducing, drawing in light
You let go, petal by petal, breaking free
One awesome, brilliant Word at a time.
You are container of more and more dew and sun.

You softness, riotous naiveté of these first days
Maturing velvet red, My God, the perfume fills the earth
And color moves the mountains of your time.
Stay, stay why do you let the bees eat?
Stay, stay why do you so loosely hold the spiral now?
Almost full circle; heart all given
Letting go again, one petal at a time
I will press you in my book of time.
As you drop into the earth you mix with brown
Your place on the tree forever scarred by the joy of you
Given back to God Who sees you and loves you forever.

This poem is about the life cycle, the stages and chapters of our lives. Each of us can perhaps, find an outline of our own story in it

All green, tight closed tiny promise of
All that will unfold in swelling.
Grace; gift who calls you out.

We take ourselves and our lives so much for granted. We just live and meet the situations of each day. Necessity pushes us on. "Just like everyone else," we think. Yet, once a year, at Christmas time so many of us watch the actor, Jimmy Stewart in a classic film, *It's a Wonderful Life*. Once a year, the television networks feel compelled to program it again. Once a year, we watch a movie about the story of a man who gets a chance to see what his world, his town, his family and friends would be like had he never lived. We see that one man's life made the difference between a thriving community and a violent, sleazy, hostile slum. One man saved and enriched innumerable lives. Why do we watch it? Because at the heart of that story is a profound truth that feeds souls. We starve for the archetypal truth that it tells: *Each of us is the only one.* There is only *one* of each of us. There is only one of me who will ever be. I am irreplaceable. I am a unique creation. I am a unique image of God.

Our stories are important, our lives make a difference. This is an ancient truth so essential to human nature that we abandon it only with peril to our sanity and souls, and the risk of living death. That archetypal idea touches every human heart. The need to find meaning in every stage of our lives is built into us. We long to believe that our lives have meaning.

We long to believe that behind, within, around each of us is a "Grace who calls us out," not just the "one damn thing after another" of our days. We have intuitions that there is more to us than our bodies. There is something spiritual about us. From the beginning, each of us is a mysterious tiny, opening bud, an individual filled with promise, a newness that will touch and unfold upon this earth. There is an inscape as well as a landscape of our lives. We have intuitions that if only we could see it from a different side we would know it. There is a spiritual and inner life to be lived as well as a material and external life.

We have lost touch with this spiritual dimension in which previous societies were immersed. Or is it that we have simply lost touch with the ways to verbalize and ritualize it? For, if in our busy lives we have lost touch with this spiritual dimension, it has not lost touch with us. This spiritual aspect of ourselves is very real. It comes built in at birth. That is why few of us can see a newborn without awakening a stirring of spirit within ourselves. Babies come, the poet Wordsworth said, "bearing wisps of other worldliness." Psychiatrist Carl Jung said in his autobiography, "I cannot tell you who or what God is, yet, through my work I have discovered the pattern of God in every person." In his book, *Timeless Healing*, Herbert Benson, MD, puts the same thought this way, "We are," he says, "hard wired for God." The human quest for meaning has always been connected to a Mysterious More, a Beyond, a Transcendent Other, a *Grace who calls us forth*.

> Bending back upside down, letting ripe red only show.
> A slit of fire, reaching out, seducing, drawing in light
> You let go petal by petal breaking free
> One awesome, brilliant Word at a time.

In these lines the poem speaks of childhood and youth. Each of us will swell and grow in these years. The story of me will swell and be told word by word as I touch so many lives and life forms. The energy of my presence lingers, each place is transformed by my presence. Scientists tell us that the sound waves that my voice and movements make are ripples, moving out and changing but never annihilated. Yet, even more, my spirit, my soul, that sacred expression of the divine that I am is eternal. That too is making its indelible mark on the universe. The gospel of John in the Christian scriptures, open with the awesome phrase, *In the beginning was the Word and the Word was with God and the Word was God. . . . And the Word was made flesh and made his dwelling among us.* These faith proclamations of John's early Christian community were about Jesus. However, it is in that same gospel where Jesus prays to God, "And the glory you gave me, I gave them, so that they may be one just as we are one" (John 17:22). Jesus is saying that we too are, though in our flawed way, an Image of God. He taught others to call God by an *intimate, familiar* name that a child uses for a parent when he suggested that they call God, as he did, "Abba." He is suggesting our intimacy with God. Each of us is an offspring, an epiphany of God. Our lives, too, speak a word about God that has never been spoken before in history. *One awesome brilliant Word at a time.*

There are deep, deep roots to my existence, genes that go back and back, and a psyche that has archetypal dimensions. There are generations of women and men who brought me forth. There are ancient ones behind me. Those lives are made more fruitful and complete by my becoming. There are young ones who will come after me. Tomorrow and tomorrow will be somehow different, richer for my having been here. Yet, my soul is mine alone, a one of a kind inbreaking of God.

From this spiritual perspective each birth is incredible. The first half of life is incredible, as petal by petal, we break free. We draw in light from the people, the events, the milieu around us. We bend toward the suns that nourish us as what is within is being led out, educated. The word educate means *to lead out that which is within.* The inner life of the spirit will become more and more manifest as I become more and more myself. God will be more and more glorified as I become more and more myself. "The glory of God is the human person fully alive," said Saint Iraeneus in the second century.

In Joan and Erik Eriksons' life cycle theory, the first and basic strength that an infant must secure as it begins ego development, is hope. The infant learns to trust the world it has entered, the people who surround it. The infant begins to learn to bear the tension between trust and mistrust. The baby learns to trust. Yet, she or he must learn to mistrust too. To be too trusting can be as dangerous as not trusting at all.

Little Philip was greatly desired by his mother and father. From the day that he was born, he was the center of their lives. "He needs me so much, I can't stand to see his frustration, the way his tiny little feet and hands curl up when he's uncomfortable. I just have to run whenever I hear him cry," Philip's new mother said on the phone. That baby was certainly learning to trust that his needs would be met, that his world was a welcoming place.

The Eriksons' point out that the baby learns to trust by experiencing having its needs met. The hungry baby stops crying when the breast or the bottle gets put in its mouth. The uncomfortable baby stops crying when it is soothed. Again and again, the baby asks with its cries and again and again, the cries are answered. Gradually, a baby may stop crying when it hears the footsteps on the way to meet its needs. It has learned that someone will come and make things better. It has begun to learn to trust. Later that same child will learn not to go with a stranger. It will learn to mistrust. Eventually, a person learns that hope is neither presumption nor despair. It is neither presumption that everyone and everything is safe and will treat me well, nor that everyone and everything is dangerous and will hurt me. Throughout life, this will be relearned again and again.

Any of us who has that kind of parenting is blessed indeed. The seductive, utter neediness of the human infant draws in the attention and care of most of the adults who encounter it. A lost child will bring out the mother archetype, the nurturer alive in almost any one of us.

Yet there are neglected and even abused children whose basic trust of the world is severely damaged by their earliest experiences. The outside environment of any of us can indeed cause many such scars to our ego. We can never make light of such painful experiences. They need to be grieved and worked through. However, we are never rendered hopelessly, irredeemably damaged because we are always more than ego. We are a spiritual Self, a Soul. Hope is a potential within us to be led out. It is unconsciously ours to be made conscious. It is a gift of our eternal spirit. In our environment there is so much to initiate and educate and touch our soul to release the archetypal motifs within us.

Perhaps what trust we have was not taught by the abusive parents who bore us. However, it was gained while sitting in a tree as a young child, looking up at translucent green leaves stretching toward a brilliant blue sky. Perhaps we began to trust while running after a seed borne on a white fluffy thing, or beneath a black star-pierced sky that stretched away forever. Perhaps, trust was born and nourished in us at the edge of an ocean that moved in and out on faithful tides. Or trust comes to us as a gift from someone who finally loves us as we are. Or hope comes when in later life we find ourselves not only alive but flourishing a year after a betrayal, or a close call with disaster. There is always the *Grace who leads us out*, given in so many ways, touching into the soul, the spirit. We are set free again and again.

Grace, Gift who calls you out. Life is spirit receiving and spirit giving. Faith, hope, and love are givens of the human child, no matter how smeared or ugly is the environment surrounding the child. They reside in the soul because they are always being given to the soul who is ultimately God's. At any point in the human journey, they can break loose and infiltrate a life. These gifts underpin our humanity. We need to believe, trust and love before we can learn anything. As life goes on these gifts may be specified as religious faith, hope, and love. Saint Paul wrote to the people of ancient Corinth, 'So faith, hope and love remain but the greatest of these is love" (1 Corinthians 13:13). Paul is referring here to life beyond death. In writing to the Romans Paul tells them, "The love of God has been poured out in our hearts by the holy Spirit that has been given to us" (Romans 5:5).

In the *Life Cycle Completed,* the Eriksons say that they were surprised to become aware that all their research into the psychological development of the human person led them to see a correspondence between the certain crucial ego strengths: trust, fidelity, love—and hope, faith, and charity.

"More specifically, if developmental considerations lead us to speak of hope, fidelity and care as the human strengths or ego qualities emerging from such strategic stages as infancy, adolescence and adulthood, it should not surprise us (though it did when we first became aware of it) that they correspond to such major credal values as Hope, Faith and Charity" (58).

The vulnerability, pliability, uncertainty, "riotous naiveté" of these early years of our lives are painful and wonderful. We break free "One awesome, brilliant Word at a time." There are desires and frustrations, joys, sorrows, glories as we move further and further into adulthood.

Maturing velvet red;
My God, the perfume fills the earth
And color moves the mountains of your time.

There is a coming now, in midlife and the mature years, to the place where we began and recognizing it again for the first time (T. S. Eliot, *Four Quartets*). That place is my Self. It is now *my* Self. I have grown into it. I have made it consciously mine, my own. Yet, it is so much more than me. It is so much more than what I am conscious of, or what I could be conscious of. The Self that I am is the image of God. It is the enfleshment of God. The tremendous contribution of the Christian era that began two thousand years ago is that it moved God definitively into humanity. Christianity said that in this man, Jesus, God was living humanly. This is an enormous expansion of human consciousness, to believe that a human being could be divine. Then Jesus' message proclaimed yet further mysterious things which our consciousness has yet fully to take in. Jesus said, "The Spirit of Truth is with you and will be within you" (John 14:17). He said, "The reign of God is in the midst of you," "The Kingdom of God is within you" (Luke 17:21). "I am in my Father, you are in me and I am in you" (John 14:20). He was telling us wondrous things about ourselves. This recognition that each of us is a revelation, a manifestation, an epiphany of God, an image of God. "Whatsoever you do to the least of my brothers and sisters, that you do to me" (Matt. 25:40). This was very much the good news of Jesus.

Christianity has uncovered divinity *in* Jesus and rightly so. His revelation of God was unclouded and definitive. For two thousand years, Christianity has struggled to hold on to the mysterious truth of both the divinity and humanity of Jesus. Yet, this same Jesus invited each person he met, no matter how lacking or sinful, or godless to recognize his or her own intimacy with God, his or her own imaging of God and to grow into that self image. He invited them to recognize themselves as offspring of God. "You too call God as I do, Father." Could he have said Mother too? He broke through so many cultural stereotypes in his dealings with women and undeniably saw them equally as revelations of God.

To reduce God completely to humanity is the height of inflation. To confine God to earth is folly. God is transcendent. God is transcendent as well as immanent; beyond, as well as within. All the great religions have held these two realities in tension. The transcendence of God is the point of Judaism's monotheism; of Christianity's Trinity, of Islam's Allah, of Buddhism's No Thing, of the native American's Great Spirit and of Hinduism's distinction between Brahman and Atman. All these religions hold on to the Transcendence of God.

Yet, at the beginning of a new millennium, there has been a tremendous movement to recapture the immanence of God; to recapture our own godliness, our own God within, the immanence and immediacy of God, the divine indwelling. There were ways in the recent past in which the transcendence of God was so emphasized that God became totally beyond the earth and the human. To many, God became irrelevant to the earth and human beings. Holocausts, genocides, and obscene violence of all kinds have been the result of this loss of the recognition of God within, of awareness of the divine spark within ourselves, and within everyone else. God seemed to be dead to most, and fearsome to those who still cared.

With the movement to recapture the God within, has come the yearning to recapture our own souls and personal spiritualities. There is a deep hunger for the recapturing of the spiritual dimension. There is a longing for finding our souls again, for reconnecting with the source and force of our being, the being who we uniquely are. The chaos of our times makes this an imperative. The second half of life makes it even more necessary, as we begin to shed the drivenness of our youthful ego. The second half of life makes it more and more real as our bodies begin a metamorphosis and our psyches open to new unconscious depths. This is the time of a new kind of generativity—a spiritual generativity; a time of passion for life, human and divine.

The Image of God that I reveal is always developing. While the body ages, my spirit is forever new. It can be forever more and more transfigured and translucent, even as I still continue to struggle with the real potential for evil within and around me.

The Soul Is Always Young

We met a wonderful eighty-two-year-old woman while we were leading a retreat for people in the second half of life in Ireland. She was French.

At seventy-eight, she had volunteered to come to Ireland to work as a receptionist in the small retreat center. She had learned English there and spoke it with a combination of a French accent and an Irish brogue. She said to us. "When I look in the mirror I say to myself, 'You are a very old woman!' But when I am not looking in the mirror, I never think of myself as an old woman. The soul, I think, is always young. Do you agree?"

The people in our programs always respond with a hearty, "yes" if we ask them her question. The other staff members of the retreat center in Ireland told us what a gift she was to them in every way: the many quiet tasks she did with such care, her peaceful presence and wit, her profound wisdom, her transforming presence to the retreatants.

The soul is always young, always filled with abundant life, always new, even while the body proclaims the weathering of the number of years lived. Martha Graham, ninety-one, told Betty Friedan (Friedan, *Fountain of Age*, 1993: 609), "The body is your instrument in dance, but your art is outside that creature. I don't leap or jump any more. I look at the young dancers and I am envious, but *more aware* of what glories the body contains. But sensitivity is not made dull by age." It was out of that sensitivity; out of her art, out of her greater awareness of the glories of the body that she was able to create some of the most beautiful dances ever performed. It was out of her spirit, out of her young soul that she generated ten new ballets after she was no longer able to dance herself. This is spirit receiving and spirit giving at this time of life.

The spiritual creativity that rises out of the movement toward wholeness at this time of life is a kind of praise—a praise of life, a praise of creation, a praise of the Source of life. In *Encore*, (1993:16) the poet, May Sarton in her eightieth year said,

> These are not hours of fire but years of praise
> The glass full to the brim, completely full
> But held in balance so no drop can spill

Betty Friedan interviewed Ida Davidoff, a psychotherapist who got her Ph.D. from Columbia at fifty-eight. The interview took place when Ida was eighty and still in practice. Ida is a wonderful example of a young soul whose spirituality flows from her, becoming more whole as she ages. She is quoted in the *Fountain of Age*, (338–39):

"The older you get, the more you like yourself. I have gained tremendously more self-confidence in the last four or five years, become more integrated as a person now, more together. My work has become more daring, more spontaneous, more effective. . . . I react as a whole person now, as my self reacting as a whole to the essence of the other person. Because you have this greater trust in yourself, your antenna picks up messages you couldn't hear before. You can't hear if you're full of your own self doubt—worrying about whether you're saying the right thing. . . . The freer I am, the more I act as a whole person—which has come with age—the more effective I am in helping people get over their anxieties. . . . If you need an excuse for not doing something, for staying put, for not risking, you use poor health, magnify it. . . . I am constantly aware that I am living on borrowed time. [She had a rare incurable immunological disease.] Yet, I live as if I'm going to live a long time. I'm putting in bulbs, planting shrubs that will take years to grow. Why deprive yourself of even an hour of beauty because you don't know if you'll be around to enjoy it?"

This is spirituality, this is soulfulness. This is faith, hope, and love. There is nothing abstract about the faith, hope, and love evidenced here. Spirituality is how we live our lives. It is the manifestation of the soul of a person, which from a religious perspective is God's work of art as well as our own.

> Maturing velvet red; My God, the perfume fills the earth
> And color moves the mountains of your time.
> Stay, stay why do you let the bees eat?
> Stay, stay why do you so loosely hold the spiral now
> Almost full circle; heart all given

Betty Friedan's book has hundreds of interviews with people in the second half of life, especially in the later years. It is a gold mine of examples of people who are realistic about aging, but who are spirit receiving and spirit giving. Time and again she finds people talking about *becoming more whole, more my own person;* Jung calls this individuation. The adventure of life's second half is to become whole, my true Self. The Self, says

Jung, is the image of God. One after the other of her interviewees speak too in different ways about a *growing spirituality*.

She quotes Norman Lear, creator of *All in the Family*, and other classic American television series. Lear was sixty-five at the time of the interview. He illustrates the move from ego to Self and acknowledges a growing spiritual side.

"I have a lot of friends my age and they're much older. They work out, play a lot of golf and tennis but they begrudge age. They can't enjoy age because they don't want to admit it. They can't accept being what and where they are. I'm beginning to deal with the reality of being older. I gave up all the trappings of office but I didn't give up the power of the person I've become. Act III feels more like a time for growing vertically, from a deeper place, a more reflective place. Act III means less fear of being found out for who I really am. Maybe I could even get to the poetic side of my nature without stuttering. I used to be afraid that my competitors and colleagues would find out that I have a *spiritual side* [italics ours]. I'm far more tolerant in my third act of other people who ask my own hidden questions, even on the opposite political side" (Friedan, 1993: 343).

Power of person . . . a deeper place . . . reflective place . . . poetic side . . . spiritual side . . . more tolerant—this is the stuff of soul life. At the time of this interview, he was busy pouring out his resources and time into organizing a group for the support of American democracy. This too is the stuff of soulmaking.

Spiritual practices, prayer, inner work, religious rituals are all important and can have a very important place in our soulmaking and spiritual life. Yet, none of these equals a person's spirituality. The spiritual dimension of a person is part of our humanity. It is a gift of God. Freud told us of our repressed sexuality but it was Jung who told us that we had repressed our spirituality. All through our lives there are intuitions, whispers, what Peter Berger called "Rumors of Angels," from this repressed spiritual side trying to break through our materialistic worldview. Norman Lear speaks for most modern people when he says that he was afraid to let his colleagues and competitors find out that he had a spiritual side. We continue this repression through the second half of life only with peril to our souls. Carl Jung said that at the root of every neurosis in his patients in the second half of life was some loss of faith. In every cure, he found that there was some recovery of religious experience. Here, of course, Jung is talking about something different from a person's religious practice. Sometimes this recovery of religious experience comes in many tiny revelations of a divine indwelling. Sometimes, such a religious experience, which is the inbreaking from our souls of their divine connection, comes like a bolt of lightning. This poem from the twentieth century Irish poet William Butler Yeats speaks of such a sudden inbreaking. Yet the setting is not a great cathedral but a crowded coffee shop.

VACILLATION

My fiftieth year had come and gone,
I sat, a solitary man,
in a crowded London shop,
An open book and empty cup
On the marble table-top.

While on the shop and street I gazed
My body of a sudden blazed;
And twenty minutes more or less
It seemed, so great my happiness,
That I was blessed and could bless.

(1983: 249)

From the outside, from a superficial perspective, age can be seen solely as diminishment. There is certainly much pain and terrible loss in the aging process. Indeed for too many people that is *all* there is. That is all they can see. Every aging person has his or her bitter complaints. It is possible for a person to totally identify him or herself with the pain and loss and *become complaint.* Yet, for most, and this often amazes younger people around them, bitterness does not consume them. The soul is always young, creating and recreating. Paradoxically, some of its greatest creation always goes on out of pain and loss. Jesus told us that it is only when a seed dies that it bears much fruit.

James Michener, the prolific novelist, who began writing novels in his forties tells a striking story of the fruit, the soulmaking that comes out of pain and loss. This story comes from his autobiography, *The World Is My Home* (3–4), which was written when he was eighty-five. Michener's story is a perfect parable for the second half of life. We will let the great storyteller tell the story himself.

> I have been impelled to attempt this project [an autobiography], because of an experience that occurred eighty years ago when I was a lad of five, and was of such powerful import that the memory of it has never left me. The farmer living at the end of our lane had an aging apple tree that had lost its energy and ability to bear fruit at all. The farmer on an early spring day, I still remember, hammered eight nails, long and rusty, into the trunk of that tree. Four were knocked in close to the ground on four different sides of the trunk, four higher up and well spaced around the circumference.
>
> That autumn a miracle happened. The tired old tree, having been goaded back to life, produced a bumper crop of juicy red apples, bigger and better than we had seen before. I asked how this had happened, the farmer explained,
>
> "Hammerin' in the rusty nails reminded it that its job was to produce apples."
>
> "Was it important that the nails were rusty?"
>
> "Maybe it made the mineral in the nail easier to digest."
>
> "Was eight important?"
>
> "If you're goin' to send a message, be sure it's heard."
>
> "Could you do the same next year?"
>
> "A substantial jolt lasts about ten years."

Michener goes on to say that in the 1980s when he was almost eighty years old, he too had some very large, rusty nails hammered into his trunk—a quintuple bypass heart surgery, a new hip, a dental rebuilding, an attack of permanent vertigo. He said that all this made him resolve to resume bearing fruit. During the next five years, he wrote eleven books. His autobiography was published when he was eighty-six. He said, "The job of an apple tree is to bear apples, I write because the job of a storyteller is to tell stories, and I have concentrated on that obligation."

It is significant that one of those stories is his own story, the story of his life. He tells us that he did not write because he feared death but because he knew who he was. He was a storyteller. He had found his meaning, his spirituality, his soul.

Aging has some rusty nails to hammer into each of us, but it also gives us the potential to bear some of the richest fruit of our lives. Aging is very difficult. Actress Katharine Hepburn once said that old age is not for sissies. We will be pierced and shocked again and again losing powers that we never even knew we had until they are taken from us. There will be real suffering. We will perhaps lose youthful vigor and beauty, strength, and agility. We will possibly lose places and things to which we have given ourselves. We will lose people, perhaps the dearest people of all. Yet, with all this, old age is not a curse, but a triumphant time.

The vintage years of each of us affect the world around us in a way that was not possible earlier. The essence of whom we have become emanates in subtle and penetrating ways. There is so much more to us to give back to the environment now; if we have used the gift of long life to become much more. Individuation, as Jung described it, is no ego trip. Life is no ego trip. It is for so much more than myself, so much more than the human race. Only God knows what mountains my life will move. Only God knows what I am ultimately all about, the mystery of my life, the colors of my unique personality.

> Almost full circle heart all given
> I will press you in my book of time.
> As you drop into earth, you mix with brown
> Your place on the tree forever scarred by the joy of you
> Given back to God Who sees you and loves you forever.

THREE

A Jungian Perspective: Insights for Long Life

Seasons of the Heart

Vital involvement, in his inner and outer life, filled Carl G. Jung's eighty-six years. His autobiography published the year he died, 1961, reveals an intense love for, and an absorption with life itself. In his mideighties he writes, "I am astonished, disappointed, pleased with myself. I am distressed, depressed, rapturous. I am all of these things at once, and cannot add up the sum" (1961:358).

Living life fully calls for involvement in our inner and outer life with all its joys, sorrows, and ordinariness. If, at times, we are called to deal with being truly disappointed with ourselves, there are other times when we can rejoice and be genuinely pleased with ourselves, as happened to Jung. If there are moments of great or even chronic distress, and if we are called at times to suffer and even enter creatively into moments or periods of depression, we can know that we have been rapturous and will be again. To be truly human is to enter into life with its highs and lows. The older person, the life-experienced person, having lived five, six, seven, eight or more decades has the resources for the acceptance of life, the reorganization of life, the embrace of life with its pain and its rapture. All these different seasons of the heart have an essential contribution to make to the ongoing generation of the soul and the maturation of the personality.

The fifty-year-old has absorbed half a century of living. She can look back upon herself in her early childhood, in her school years, in adolescence and recapture what it was like for her at that time. She can reflect on how she grew, what she learned, how she matured. A man of fifty, sixty, or seventy years can look back at his own youth and reexperience the time between childhood and youth. He can recall the sexual stirring, the feelings of power and uncertainty, the failures and successes, the events and the cop-outs. He can relive his twenties and thirties, long gone.

The older men and women can recall the first stirring of midlife, the early season of discontent and hopefully, a new blossoming of person, a fuller maturation, and a growing ability to deal with ambiguity and contradiction. Having a living creative sense of one's history allows one to own the present as well as the past and the future, and to experience oneself as a whole.

These new years, these later decades of pure gift, call for a greater inner and outer freedom, a centering of one's self, a reorientation of one's very own being, a journeying inward to the exploration of one's own inner space, and a rechanneling of energy to explore a new world. Only the increased consciousness possible with an addition of years can allow someone to see and experience so much. "See it all and be not afraid." Before "one had eyes, but could not see; ears but could not hear or understand" (Matthew 13:13). In the Christian Scripture Christ, the archetype of the Self, speaks to us in the light of Isaiah's prophecy about healing and wholeness. "But blest are your eyes because they see and blest are your ears because they hear" (Matthew 13:15). Jung's theory of personality development is a lens that helps us to see more of what we have lived, and to understand and evoke the development toward individuation and wholeness to which life's second half invites us.

There is a terrible busyness about life's first half. We are busy preparing to be grown up and then even busier being grown-up. As we were molded day by day in our mother's womb, so too, are we molded in childhood, adolescence, early and later youth, as well as in our midlife transition and our early midlife years when we are "in our prime"—the great caretakers of the world, and of the younger and older generations. But as we move into our sixth and seventh decades, our psyche begins to make even stronger demands to experience the Self in a new way. The very soul and body of the older man and woman cries out for a unification and a cessation of terribly busyness and frenetic activity.

In his seventy-eighth year, the famous teacher, author, and anthropologist Joseph Campbell said: "The forty-year-old should see himself as an independent, self-responsible human being with free will. And he should have certain noble powers of the heart that have been called to his attention and to which he has been invited to give himself that will enable him to act in terms of nobility, not in obedience, but out of himself. On the other hand, the older person must know, 'I'm now not participating in the achievement of life. I have achieved it.' Personally, in my own life I am now looking back, and I can tell you that there's a wonderful moment that comes when you realize, 'I'm not striving for anything. What I'm doing now is not a means to achieving something later.' Youth has always to think that way. Every decision young people make is a commitment to a life course, and, if they make a bad decision, by the time they get down the road, they're far off course. But after a certain age, there's not a future, and suddenly the present becomes rich, it becomes that thing in itself which you are now experiencing" (1989:94–95).

Yet perhaps life's first half so overextended us in our outer environment and things external that we come to this new stage in the dark about our own greater inner wealth and resources. Perhaps we come to our fifties and beyond, blind to the depths that can cradle our aging, redirect our energy, refound a genuine sense of Self, regenerate our soul and shift our course from ego development to the becoming of the Self. This is the real, great work of a lifetime that makes pale all the achievement of life's first half. And the soul recycles everything in its recreation. No pain, diminishment, failure, loss, sorrow is cast off. Everything is used in the spinning of the new being, born again and again fifty, sixty, seventy, eighty, ninety, one hundred.

The Unconscious in Jung's Theory of Personality Development

It was Sigmund Freud and Carl Jung who in the first half of the twentieth century brought the existence and the importance of the unconscious to our attention. In Jung's view, we had lost an awareness of our own unconscious inner depths, and were not harnessing its great potentials for a dynamic, healthy, more conscious living. Yet at the same time, these unconscious depths were too often not dormant but wreaking havoc in people's lives. We had come to believe that we were what we appeared to ourselves and others to be.

We equated ourselves with the ego or our consciousness of ourselves, yet, growing up, we repress all kinds and varieties of parts of ourselves. If for example mother and dad wanted you always to be a "happy camper," you repressed and denied any discontent, moodiness, or just plain mellowness, no less boredom, and sadness or anger. It had its advantages. Still being perceived a happy camper at thirty or fifty, you could list them. Yet, at the same time, you also repressed and denied real parts of yourself that robbed you of some of life's richness. You are still running from, hiding from, any sad or unpleasant situation. You still have to make a joke in every instance and out of everything. You cannot believe anyone will love you if you get serious or sad or angry. Worst of all, you do not even know you do these things. You do not know you are still at thirty-seven or fifty-seven trying always to be a "happy camper."

Where do these repressed parts of yourself go? Can they be resurrected? If so, will they enrich your life? Will they unseat your ego? Will you be a stranger to yourself and others? Your psyche has been housing all the repressed aspects of yourself in your unconscious. Surely to your shock and surprise some have already disrupted your life by rising uncontrollably and wielding their power. Sometime in midlife the "happy camper" will begin to have fierce black moods or even severe depression, if the midlife person has not yet begun to let the serious side take its place in his/her personality. We can be sure that the education the unconscious can give us will keep us busy and fascinated for all of life's second half. But sometimes, the tuition can be costly.

These are the years for the exploration of our inner space. These are the years for reclaiming lost, unknown, unused, unconscious aspects of myself. The psyche demands this of me. The life cycle created the time and situation for this flowering of the personality, for individuation, that is, for becoming the unique and whole person I am called to be. This is archetypal. The human person is programmed for this reorientation. It is built in. True, archetypal or not, this life developmental stage can go awry and often does.

Jung saw the unconscious psyche, the collective unconscious, as well as the personal unconscious as the creative bed. My personal unconscious is uniquely my own. It is here that I can find all that I have unconsciously repressed or consciously suppressed, all that I have unconsciously forgotten or never brought to consciousness. It is here that every detail of my story is collected. Re-member-ing is a human capacity, a gift giving us depth, history, roots, continuity, and a unified spirit moving us toward Soul and wholeness.

How is it that having never thought of my graduation day from grade school, and whenever asked, not being able to recall it, suddenly thirty or fifty years later, some little event brings it to my memory as though it were yesterday? Why can a seventy-year-old, when asked to recall the first book she ever read, respond that she has no idea? Yet, an hour later, she returns and says with delight, "I remember. It was, *Black Beauty.*"

Visiting a ninety-five-year-old aunt who had been born in Ireland, her niece, who lived halfway across the United States and rarely saw her aunt, was describing the old woman's birthplace. She had recently returned from her tenth trip to Ireland and had a great knowledge of that country. She had spent hours absorbing her own parents' stories of the old country. Her aunt was delighted. She had long been cut off from the rest of her siblings by distance and then death. She had never returned to the Ireland she left in her youth. Questioning her aunt about her mother, the niece's grandmother, brought wonderful new stories. Then the old woman sang a song that her mother had composed and sung eighty-five years before. "It's the first time I've sung that song since I was ten years old!" she said. "It's so good to talk about all this, you know. I've been spending a lot of time back there these days."

Where have these lost fragments of the story been? They are stored in our own depths, our psyche, named by Jung the personal unconscious. More amazing still is the fact that the personal unconscious is not always dormant. Unconscious, yes; inactive, no. Unknown to us, we may be acting and choosing because of our unconscious story. The personal unconscious is a powerhouse determining much of the script we live, even as our conscious ego informs the same script.

For example, a man may find a natural distrust of women has come to characterize his adult ego, affecting his personal and professional relationships with women and many of the decisions he makes. It goes back to the first woman in his life, his mother. When he was twenty months old, his young mother died. Being abandoned by his mother has created an unconscious, innate fear of abandonment by other women, and a very conscious distrust permeating any attempts at good rapport.

Can he not now finally, in the second half of life and after so many experiences with women, begin to recognize not only the pattern, but the roots of the pattern? Can he not finally reparent and reassure this little boy within him that every woman is not going to abandon him? Growth in consciousness makes this a real possibility.

Another man made a profession of the military. Joining the military at eighteen, he found himself thirty years later preparing for retirement. Only forty-eight, retirement for him meant searching for a new career. He wanted something totally different and unconnected to the work he had zealously given himself to in the first half of life. He started to explore his options four years before his retirement date. Vacationing at different resorts during that decade gave him the opportunity of having a body massage. Eventually, he talked to one of the professionals about the training he needed to become a licensed massage therapist. He thought, "This is what I'll do." He searched out the best training and signed himself into the program at the end of his first free year. This was an amazing choice for a "military man." An amazing choice for a man who had shared with all of us at a Mid-Life Directions Workshop the following facts about his personal childhood.

"One of my earliest memories is of myself at four or five sitting on my grandfather's lap," he told us. "He was holding me and rocking me." This recollection made him fill up with gratitude because, as he told us, "As I look back, my grandfather was the only one who ever held me." Here we have a man bringing his tired body to a resort and enjoying an invigorating massage. He feels the benefits of body contact and chooses becoming a massage therapist as his second career. How affected was this choice of his by this early experience? Starved for touch, starved for holding and hugging, he remembered appreciatively the times when his grandfather held him. Now, he chooses to become licensed to touch others.

A woman searched for a home and settled on three wonderful houses in ideal locations. She was having a difficult time coming down on a final choice and selection. Finally, a felt sense makes her come down on one particular house. "I'm not sure why," she said. "I really love all three, but I can only take one. This one feels most right." The house is surrounded by a lovely piece of landscape covered with old, gracious evergreen trees. Growing up rather poor, her parents did everything to make Christmas a happy time. Christmas wreaths and a Christmas tree made this family feast more memorable. Her father used his truck to bring evergreens down from upstate and sell them in the city. He always chose an especially beautiful tree for the family, and its evergreen smell filled the house at Christmas time. It was at the heart of their merriment. The aroma of spruce had come to symbolize the best of family life as well as the presence of comforting care whether from loving others or a loving God. In choosing the home with evergreen trees, this woman was in her selection of a home unconsciously making a choice for re-creating the best in home life. Always at our disposal, the personal unconscious disturbs and enriches our daily lives.

Florida Scott-Maxwell was born in Florida in 1883. In 1910, she married and went to live in her husband's native Scotland where she raised her family. At fifty, in 1933, she began training as a Jungian analyst under Carl Jung. Florida's later midlife years were filled with activity: practicing in Scotland and England, working for woman's suffrage, authoring plays and books and "tending to her children and flowers." Jung's wife, Emma, the mother of five, also became an analyst in her midlife years. This certainly reflects one of Jung's great contributions to women's psychology. Jung early on recognized the creative and generative aspects of women aside from that of being wife and mother. In many ways, he helped prepare the way for the women's movement and the study of women's and men's psychology that is so much a part of the present time.

In Florida Scott-Maxwell's later years, she kept a journal that she called "Her Notebooks." She died in 1979 at the age of ninety-seven. Her notebooks were published as a unique kind of autobiography. We are blessed to have her reflections on living the mature years in *The Measure of My Days*. These lines from her book speak so well of the activity of the unconscious: "Ideas drift in like bright clouds, arresting, but they come as visitors. A shaft of insight can enter the back of my mind and when I turn to greet it, it is gone. I did not have it, it had me. My mood is light and dancing, or it is leaden. It is not I who choose my moods; I accept them, but from whom?" (1979:19).

The Collective Unconscious:
Gifts from the Inner Sea

There is another creative dynamic force beyond one's own personal unconscious and that is the inherited, collective patterns of the human race. There is human psychic equipment, that is more than personal, which is part of each human person. At our birth, our human psyche is not an empty or a clean slate. It is a creative ferment filled with the seeds of human possibilities, potentials, and archetypal motifs from which one's uniqueness will flow and from which new life will be born again and again in one's lifetime. Jung called it the "objective psyche" or the "collective unconscious." These are ways of being and relating, growing and becoming, the unconscious substratum of the human person from which life flows consciously or unconsciously. These archetypes of the collective unconscious are like the instincts in animals. When the archetypal *teacher* arose in Martha Graham, it was her collective unconscious that released, in the midst of her coma, and at the precise moment in that precise situation, the power, ability, and desire to teach others. She had taught before, but dancing, not teaching, had characterized her very life.

Have you experienced the archetypal Teacher, that human ability to teach, inherent in your own depths, coming forward and taking a place in your life? Have you taught someone to bake bread, to whistle, to catch a ball, to enjoy classical music, to theologize, to change a tire? Did you take your teaching power and make a profession out of it? Or have you enjoyed teaching as part of a larger profession, i.e., being a doctor, lawyer, paraprofessional, mechanic? The archetypal Teacher came alive in Martha Graham and resurrected her personally and professionally.

An actor, like Ronald Reagan, may find the archetype of *public servant* arise in him or her. In the film *Hero*, Dustin Hoffman plays a sleazy no-good who has the *hero* arise in him. On the other hand, anyone of us trying to live a good life may find the *thief* or *murderer* wake up in him or her. Nevertheless, Jung says, that all growth comes from the unconscious in the second half of life. The collective unconscious is a bed of creativity, nourishing us in all the stages of life. It is not dried up in midlife or in old age. It may be dammed or blocked, but engineered by the Self, it can push itself forth as it did with Martha Graham. Our unconscious is like an ocean, a vast sea teeming with life. It has many gifts to give us. Look for and expect gifts from this sea. There are thousands of archetypes. One may suddenly experience a dormant Mother, Father, Trickster, Solitary, Clown, Sage, Teacher, Poet, or Hero rise in oneself or another.

We know that in his old age Albert Einstein regretted that he had neglected his feeling side and that he had not read much poetry in his lifetime. The discovery of poetry, his joy in poetry readings, and this regret about his past is evidence of an awakening in himself. He began to value a neglected, repressed aspect of his own psychic equipment. Indeed, this part of him had been awakened, and his regret is giving acknowledgement and honor to an aspect of his own psyche that had come to consciousness.

The American president Theodore Roosevelt, is noted for the "manly pursuits." He fostered his personal ideal of manhood in his own sons. One son, Quentin, killed in World War I, brought to the aging Teddy a painful realization. He wondered if his own glorification of manly heroism had contributed to his son's death. A flood of feeling and sentiment opened up his heart and he began to treasure life and his grandchildren in a new way. The pain of his loss with the death of his son and the realization of his own possible participation in that death opened him up to release a whole set of more gentle, culturally, feminine human qualities until then repressed, unconscious and disdained. We each have within us a powerhouse of resources awaiting the opportunity to enrich our lives.

THE GUEST HOUSE

by Rumi

This being human is a guest house.
Every morning is a new arrival.

A joy, a depression, a meanness,
some momentary awareness comes
as an unexpected visitor.

Welcome and entertain them all!
Even if they're a crowd of sorrows,

who violently sweep your house
empty of its furniture,
still, treat each guest honorably.
He may be clearing you out
for some new delight.

The dark thought, the shame, the malice,
meet them at the door laughing,
and invite them in.
Be grateful for whoever comes,
because each has been sent
as a guide from beyond.

The Essential Rumi (translated by
Coleman Barks)

Among Carl Jung's many dream images there was an old wise mythological man that he named Philemon. Jung spent many hours working with this dream image from his unconscious depths. In imagination, he walked and talked with Philemon as he would with any wise tutor in his outer world. This personification and amplification of a dream image is called the inner work of "active imagination." It is a method of cultivating the power of the unconscious to interact with you, harness its creative energy and enter into your growth and transformation. It was Jung's dialogue with Philemon, or his active imagination with Philemon, that clarified for him the objective psyche as the common substratum of the psyche or the inherited psychic bed of the human person. We have solidarity with one another because we share our common humanity, the basic collective unconscious and creative bed of archetypal human life, motifs, myths, art, and culture itself. Speaking of Philemon in his autobiography, he says:

> Philemon and other figures of my fantasies brought home to me the crucial insight that there are things in the psyche which I do not produce, but which produce themselves and have their own life. Philemon represented a force which was not myself. In my fantasies I held conversations with him, and he said things which I had not consciously thought. For I observed clearly that it was he

who spoke, not I. He said I treated thoughts as if I generated them myself, but in his view thoughts were like animals in the forest, or people in a room, or birds in the air, and added, "If you should see people in a room, you would not think that you had made those people, or that you were responsible for them." It was he who taught me psychic objectivity, the reality of the psyche. Through him the distinction was clarified between myself and the object of my thought. He confronted me in an objective manner, and I understood that there is something in me which can say things that I do not know and do not intend, things which may even be directed against me (1961:183).

Models of Life Movement

The life story of the famous Trappist monk, Thomas Merton, vividly portrays the process of individuation. Merton's ego development in his twenties and thirties called for taking on the role of the monk, as one set aside and apart from others, to be exclusively for God. He saw his vocation as a call to be solitary, contemplative, unworldly, "out of the world." But the greater Self is in relationship to God, and all that is of God, all of creation. The call to contemplation that Merton experienced is a common archetypal call, part of the human equipment of all people. The unparalleled sale of Merton's autobiography and all his books reveals that his experience struck a chord in other people. His books resonated in people from all walks of life and spiritual traditions.

The time came when Merton's interest and vocation began to be informed by the opposite human values from his initial ideals when he went off to be a monk. How could he still be a genuine monk characterized by solitariness and be connected to others? How could he move from total dedication to prayer and contemplation and at the same time become actively involved in the great social and cultural mutations and transformations of the day? In the nineteen sixties that included the civil rights movement, a nonviolent stance against evils, and an antiwar mentality. How could he live out his unique vocation as a contemplative and actively engage in, even ignite the archetypal contemplative in others? He had a growing sense, an archetypal sense of the common vocation of all people. As a contemplative, he had an experiential sense of solidarity and unification with others. He began to write about, befriend and counsel the activists, many of whom wrote to and visited him in his monastery.

The last two decades of his life were spent involved in this great task of individuation based upon the integration of his conscious and his emerging unconscious personality. The ideals that characterized his earlier ego had to make room for, stretch and expand to include the vast energies that evolved from his unconscious depths. He had to find how he could creatively honor the archetype of writer, world citizen, monk, universal mystic, cultural explorer, social critic, prophet, cultural transformer, intimate friend and still maintain the contemplative and solitary aspects of himself. How could these varied aspects of himself not detract from the initial person he was in the process of becoming but add to, enrich and embolden the Self in all its uniqueness?

In his fifties, Merton went to Asia to explore with the contemplatives of the east and west, the common mystical experience that unites us all. This was a giant step for humanity that Merton, among many others, took. The experience of solidarity with others is key to the soulmaking of life's second half. Merton saw in the mystical tradition of all the great religions a common, universal, human experience and moved to explore and acclaim that universality that makes us one. This was a far cry from his early days when he went off to find God in a silent Trappist monastery, away from others, away from the world. Still, that leaving the world, was an initial part of following "his bliss," and an important stage in his earlier development. In his forties and fifties, he moved into a more inclusive spirituality. Soul making in midlife and the mature years requires a great expansion of the mind and heart. This expansion is built in, and demands one's cooperation for the new growth in personality called for in the second half of life.

Again and again Thomas Merton was asked during his life to engage another aspect of his own archetypal unconscious, as living life and life situations stirred up and released vital new energies. The challenge for him was how to engage these gifts of the spirit so that their fruit would be integral to the life story he was living out. As a radical call to concern and action for the contemporary social needs of peace and justice arose in his consciousness, he could have relinquished his total dedication to a contemplative life. He could have pitted these two polarities one against another. However, instead he bore the tension of these major polarities of life itself, allowed contemplation to inform social action and social concern to feed into his contemplation. He did not choose one over the other. He did not identify with the contemplative way of life and deny the call to action. He did not identify with his call to action and allow his contemplative ego to collapse.

The becoming of the Self demands that the unconscious energies become conscious in some way and interact with the ego in a transformation to the greater self. Merton could have relinquished his contemplative life in the Christian tradition in a Trappist monastery and surrendered himself to a Buddhist, Eastern way of life. But instead, the great gift he gave us was to grow in admiration and respect for Buddhism and to have a genuine mutual relationship and exchange with that tradition and its members. To collapse one's ego ideal, identifying with the emerging powers and then exclusively live out the newly discovered values is not beneficial to the great task of becoming one's Self. It is also detrimental to have an ego so tight and enclosed that no opposing unconscious elements can find their way to consciousness. Wholeness requires dealing with mystery, paradox, uncertainty, suffering, and contradiction. There is no easy way to wholeness. No easy way to individuation.

This is not to say that many people do find that a newly emerging aspect of themselves demands radical changes in lifestyles, commitments, vocations, marriages, relationships, etc. Nevertheless, it is usually in the best interest of the Self to bear the tensions of opposing values, as a means toward the transformation of the Self. When, and if radical change is finally undertaken, following reflective soul searching, the hope is that the Self is at the heart of this demand to relinquish what was once chosen, rightly or wrongly, as the way.

Jung wrote in *Two Essays on Analytical Psychology:*

> The transition from morning to afternoon of life means a revaluation of the earlier values. There comes the urgent need to appreciate the value of the opposite of our former ideals to perceive the error in our former convictions, to recognize the untruth in our former truth, and to feel how much antagonism and even hatred lay in what until now had passed for love. Not a few of those who are drawn into the conflict of opposites jettison everything that has

seemed to them good and worth striving for; they try to live in complete opposition to their former ego. Changes of profession, divorces, religious convulsions, apostasies of every description are the symptoms of this swing over to opposites. The snag about a radical conversion into one's opposite is that one's former life suffers repression and thus produces just as unbalanced a state as existed before when the counterparts of the unconscious virtues and values were still repressed and unconscious. . . . It is, of course, a fundamental mistake to imagine that when we see the non-value in the value or the untruth in the truth, the value or the truth ceases to exist. It has only become relative. (1966:75)

Thomas Merton found that the contemplative and mystical experience that characterized his vocation was an archetypal human experience that people from all ages and traditions had experienced and practiced. Each of us has within ourselves the archetypal pattern of the solitary and the contemplative. We too have the inbuilt human equipment to be a solitary, to be a contemplative and to allow mysticism to inform and enrich us, at this time in our life. These spiritual powers may not characterize who we are, our conscious personality. They may seem totally foreign to us at the present time. They may in fact have been completely absent in the first half of life. Yet, now the contemplative and solitary may be rising in us for the first time. Initially, they may close us off from others and move us away from involvement with people and our outer world. But genuine contemplation will always eventually move us to a greater compassion for ourselves and others. Contemplation includes taking a long, attentive, patient, loving look at what is. And this loving look leads to social concern and social action. One finds a natural rhythm between solitude and involved concern for others.

Contemplation and solitude can arise in us, and transform us and our life, introducing us to our greater depths and spiritual capacities. We may come to know in a most unique way, the one we call God, "She Who Is" like Elizabeth Johnson, or like Paul Tillich, the one we call God or "The Ground of Being." We may find ourselves moving into a most profound solidarity with nature and with people of other races, religions, and traditions.

Poetry is the expression of contemplation. The Archetypal Poet in each of us sees the depths, meaning, and beauty in things. When the Archetypal Poet arose in Peggy Guditus, as we demonstrated earlier, she responded, accepting the invitation, engaging her poet and giving time and energy to the new found part of herself.

› President Jimmy Carter wrote poetry when he was in high school, and again he wrote poetry while courting his wife Rosalynn. Trained as an engineer in the scientific method, poetry tapped into a whole other side of him. For long periods of his life, the poet within him did not write poetry. But surely the poet expressed himself in his relationships, in his spiritual life, the way he saw humanity, and perhaps even in his presidency. A wonderful model of vital living and of diversity in the mature years, Jimmy Carter published his first book of poetry when he was seventy-one. *Always a Reckoning* reveals that the Archetypal Poet had made a claim on him once again. President Carter took time for poetry even while he was deeply involved in his role of international statesman and diplomat, a worker and organizer in Habitat for Humanity, The Carter Center, teaching Sunday School, etc., these were all Soul making activities for him.

However, Poetry allows President Carter to contact the deepest unknown levels of his own Soul. For this citizen of the world, poetry is the vehicle revealing his most profound humanity. In the poem "Always a Reckoning," we see him contemplating his relationship with his long deceased father. By doing so, he comes to a heightened understanding, not only of his father but of himself. This understanding of himself is not only of the young boy and man he was when his father lived, but of who he is right here, right now. We too may find the Archetypal Poet in ourselves. We may start writing poetry as Peggy Guditus and Jimmy Carter did, or we may just find ourselves looking at life with a poet's eye. This new kind of contemplative looking will feed the Soul.

A famous French fashion stylist, Nicolede Vesian, made a dramatic change of life at seventy. She took all her gifts, talents, and creativity, and became a landscape architect. She created each garden she created with a unique, compelling style. There is something contemplative in gardening. Many extroverts, in particular, as well as introverts, find it a natural, soothing, and satisfying way of turning from the outer projects to a more solitary and contemplative mode of being. Designing space, gardening the earth itself, is a most wonderful form of Soul making, as well as a great metaphor for the making of a Soul.

As Nicolede Vesian moved into her eightieth year and ninth decade, this still, magnetic, and energetic woman was optimistic about turning her energies into yet another novel venture. As she left behind the life of fashion in her seventies, she later on left behind her landscape artistry and moved into a new way of forging not only her own Soul but that of others and experiencing "the last of life for which the first was made." The fashion stylist and landscape artist became an architect of her own aging process. C. G. Jung's "four stages of life" point to this kind of expansion of personality in the second half of life. Each stage calls for its own kind of unique growth and development. Each stage has its own joys and sorrows. Each stage demands change, reorientation and expansion for the critical Soul making of that season of life.

We find the same kind of enlargement in New York's fashion designer, Bill Blass. He was seventy-two years old when we were introduced to him and his story in an interview on public television. We found his story, as told in this interview, fascinating. Like most children of his era, Blass spent Saturdays at the movie theater. It was there that this child from Fort Wayne, Indiana, became mesmerized by all the costumes parading on the screen. That Saturday life was powerfully important for this little boy as it opened him to a larger landscape filled with exciting possibilities. When Bill was five, his father, a hardware store owner, took his own life, and his mother never remarried, leaving him without a father figure at home.

The movies awakened his innate gift for sketching and design and gave him his life goal. He wanted to be in New York City, the fashion center of the country where all this intense, glamorous life he saw on the films existed. When he graduated from high school at eighteen, New York City welcomed the boy from Fort Wayne. Within a few years, he was a fashion designer and moving quickly toward the time when he owned his own fashion house.

As Charlie Rose, a skillful television interviewer, interviewed Bill Blass, we saw a man in the late midlife, or early mature years, developing the other side of his personality, although still passionately involved with his fashion world. When asked what he "liked best about his world right now," he did not refer to his life's work—fashion. He answered, "Well, I like my dogs and going to the country. I have to be perfectly honest with you, I love New York, but it's a tough city now. I prefer—God, maybe it's age, I don't know, but I really do love going to the country and staying quietly in my country home. . . . I choose to be alone now. It's the kind of—it's the ultimate freedom."

Finding solace in the solitude of the country was obviously a new venture for this intensely involved senior executive. This is the integration of his own unlived contemplative and solitary archetypal world. In life's first half, Bill's ego development was centered around the fashion world that he loved. His total dedication rewarded him and he is recognized as one of America's greatest designers. His work in the fashion world won for him the Lifetime Achievement Award from the Council of Fashion Designers.

Now, this call and response to a quieter, solitary, contemplative mode of being is a natural developmental change at this time in his life. This new growth is coming from his undeveloped side or his shadow side. Bill Blass is integrating his neglected, unconscious side on the way to becoming whole.

Bill's success has allowed him to accumulate great wealth. Yet, even here, we find a remarkable and appropriate change. He celebrated his career by donating $10 million to the New York Public Library. When asked why he did it he explained whence this philanthropy came:

> Well, it's because I've always been fascinated by books. As a kid growing up in Indiana during the Depression, books were a tremendously important part of my life, and then when I became associated with the New York Public Library here before I even joined the board, I felt terribly comfortable about the place and the people in it. It seems to me that this is something we must support. . . . that everybody must give back to the community something that they take out, and it's a miracle, I was able to do it.

New York City had welcomed the eighteen-year-old Bill Blass and opened him to innumerable opportunities to fulfill his dream in the fashion world. He followed "his bliss," in Joseph's Campbell's words, and applied himself. He had arrived in New York City with no money but a burning love and New York City cooperated with this young, enthusiastic, dedicated, creative, and hardworking young man. All of this was good ego development but now the unconscious, unlived aspects are coming alive and entering into his ongoing personality development. He experiences solidarity with the New York masses; the poor, the newcomers, the ordinary citizens and finds a way of giving to them and in sharing his legacy with the city itself.

This enlargement of personality and diversity of interest flows from "the second personality," Jung's "personality number two," and the Greater Self. Personality two is at home in the contemplative mode and solitude, and this contact with the person's inner depths and resources initiates and opens the door to a greater solidarity with others. Developmentally, there is a call to this other side of the personality, gift to the Self, and gift to the world.

We may each have an image of the solitary or contemplative person as being aloof, unconnected and unconcerned. But in these four examples of Merton, Carter, Vesian, and Blass, we see the natural incorporation of the solitary, contemplative aspects of the personality in partnership with the activity and concern for others. At the heart of contemplation is a sense of solidarity with nature, the universe, God, and peoples. Genuine contemplation leads ultimately to God, and to unification and solidarity with others, and generates an active concerned participation in caring for the world and caring for people. This is prayerful living and living prayer. It is significant that President Carter's life demonstrates so well the bearing of the tensions and the balancing of the polarity of activity and contemplation. His book of poetry was published in the same year in which Carter made three highly publicized international interventions as statesman in crisis situations in the world: Bosnia, North Korea, and Haiti.

People like Peggy Guditus, Bill Blass, Joseph Campbell, Our Monsignor, Nicolede Vesian, Martha Graham, Thomas Merton, and Joan and Erik Erikson, contribute uniquely to an urgent task at this moment in history—redefining the aging process. Aging is not about obsession with youth, aging is about continued growth and development; it is about staying productive through all the phases of life. In the later midlife years as well as in the mature years, being productive is not materialistic but generative and spiritual with regard to one's Self and with regard to the larger community, humanity itself.

FOUR

The Shadow as Gold

Know Thyself

Having a working knowledge of one's psyche and how it operates is as important as having a working knowledge of one's own digestive system, circulatory system, etc., but just as we may avoid the detailed study of some aspect of our anatomy until we, or someone we love, has a medical problem, so we too, let pass any serious study of the psyche until a problem arises. Psychic disturbances are usually a sign of a spiritual disfunction, an inordinate or insufficient use of a psychic power or delayed growth in an intellectual, emotional, spiritual, or affective mode of being. They can be seen as the signs pointing us to a richer, more fruitful way of being. Psychic disturbances often proclaim that something is going awry in our own development or the environment around us.

Throughout life, one needs to stop and see, if indeed, one's life reflects being true to oneself. One must see and hear the inner voice, the soul, the inner tune and be true to the Self, that unique image of God that I am.

At times of major transitions, like the movement from youth to midlife, one often experiences a disharmony and a dismemberment that is a call for growth in consciousness and a change in life. The felt psychic disturbance is nature's way of calling a person to stop, pay attention, discover what is amiss and make the called-for changes. Although dramatic changes can occur at any time in adult life, no time ushers in more dramatic changes than the end of youth. As one's youth comes to an end, just as when childhood came to an end, unknown and dormant aspects of the personality awaken. The end of youth awakens in us other aspects of who we are that demand acknowledgment and in some way, a place in our life.

As youth comes to an end, consciously or unconsciously, one begins to evaluate the choices made in youth. You may have chosen to marry or not to marry. Now you begin to rethink or perhaps even regret that choice. "Why did I think marriage wasn't for me? Now, if I marry my chances for a family are nil. I didn't know that the day would come when I would regret not having built a lasting relationship, a home and family with someone." Another person regrets what appears now to be a loveless marriage. "I never really loved you from the start," he or she says to an astonished wife or husband. Still another person takes the steps to leave a marriage that indeed has been loveless for the past twenty years. The situation has been so detrimental and dangerous that he/she seizes the courage that has evaded him/her before this moment. In another instance a woman cries out with real tears, regret, and pain, "I will never have my own child. Why did I let this pass me by? How could I have been so foolish?" This "sin against nature" can turn into a deep and profound mourning.

Professional people, lawyers, doctors, teachers can come to regret the choices they made, the years of study and the present weariness of what at one time they passionately embraced. Unskilled laborers and home-makers can regret the education they never got or the jobs they never pursued.

Fidelity to life commitments challenges one's feelings of being too tightly enclosed in a situation and dissatisfied with choices made too long ago. Sometimes radical changes are called for, but just as often one is being called, not to leave a marriage bed or marriage or a major career or vocational choice, but to allow the undeveloped parts of oneself to emerge and enter into a redefinition of one's goals, and a new creative design for one's life, one's marriage, one's vocation or career.

Today's midlife adult has a built-in clock that still expects life to end around forty-seven, as it did for most people at the beginning of the twentieth century. The adult psyche has not caught up with the increased life expectancy of the twenty and twenty-first centuries. Many people experience a great depression at the time of a fortieth or fiftieth birthday because of this. One's psyche expects an end to life. It takes a while, even years to know in one's own depths that today we are called to choose life again and again in life's second half. We are called again and again to rediscover our passion for life. For most of us, the greatest growth goes on in the midlife and the mature years.

Bob, as I shall call him, was a successful lawyer in a large Manhattan firm. He was happily married. He and his wife had worked at their marriage. When she got involved in being more liberated, he went along with her. He took on chores around the house and even learned to enjoy cooking. He welcomed the lively conversation they now had, mostly because of her return to college to get a degree. They had three delightful daughters and he had taken to parenting easily. But now that they were all in their teens, he found himself getting stressed out in their company. He constantly laid down the law to them about their life, friends, clothes, etc. One by one, the girls began avoiding him. They learned to sneak in and out without his knowing and because of his growing sternness and judgmental attitude, they became secretive and even easy liars. Bob's earlier happy relationship with his three daughters had deteriorated.

At the same time Bob found a bizarre thing happening to him. Every woman at work began to be undressed in his imagination. Women on the street, women clients, women in the courtroom, were all seen partly or totally naked. He had a happy sex life with his wife, but had never been oversexed. Even in his youth, unlike most of his friends, he had remained celibate until he married. He had never had another woman, other than his wife.

Bob's imaginative undressing of women he saw turned to a constant uncontrollable fantasizing of women in different degrees of nakedness. He began to be alarmed. At his church, he was on friendly terms and had great respect for his pastor. Bob remembered hearing that he had a degree in pastoral counseling but never gave much attention to the fact. Over the years, he had occasions of hearing someone praise the pastor for his counseling skills. He decided to share this embarrassing and annoying phenomenon that had suddenly crept up on him. The pastor listened as Bob explained what was happening with the erotic and obscene viewing of women. He asked many questions. Then they got to how things were going at home. Bob expressed his worry about the girls. Would one get raped? Would one get pregnant? Would they allow themselves to be taken advantage of? What about AIDS? The pastor knew the girls. They were beautiful, charming young women. Good girls. Why was Bob so extreme in his concern over them? Why had he allowed his concern to ruin his relationship with each of them?

Bob talked about his own sexual self. He admitted he wondered what sex would be like with other women. He had never brought that to consciousness before. He admitted that he wondered why he had been so conservative and traditional in his own sexual mores as a young man. Would being more sexually adventuresome now make him more exciting? He was bored with his own well-developed career. His wife was exploring new parts of herself, developing and changing.

Bob made ten other visits to the pastor. His own unconscious sexual self was revealed more and more. As he got in touch with his own horniness, Bob relaxed. He found himself getting less stressed out with the girls. He secretly went off to a few "adult movies."

He only needed a few, for a few good laughs at himself and his own parochialism. He gradually began enjoying the company of the girls again. He became less of a lawmaker and judge and a little more of a dad. His wife, especially, began to find Bob different. Their routine sex life that had become customary and minimally satisfying became more adventuresome, and they each found themselves looking forward to exploring and being different and exciting.

The budding sexuality of his young women daughters had provoked in Bob a latent and unconscious and unexplored, unconventional sexual self. Bob had projected his unconscious fear of this onto his girls. An overemotional reaction that is out of character is often the sign of a projected shadow, your own unconscious stuff. Bob's fear of promiscuity in his daughters was a fear of his own unconscious promiscuity. Getting in touch with his own sexual self opened Bob to growth in personality and relationship on many other levels. A creeping midlife ennui, as well as the possibility of damaging deviant behavior and a catastrophic collapse of his ego was curtailed and a new zest for living opened other doors. When a shadow personality awakens in us we can collapse our ego and live it out or we can hold on until we find the gold in that shadow.

Unfinished Business

At any point in our adult life, a person can wake up to the realization that the movement from childhood to adult life was never really completed. Perhaps the person chose a profession, became economically independent, but in other ways remained wedded to that first family in a limiting way. In other instances, a person may have sacrificed too great a part of himself or herself, in an effort toward adaptation in a family, marriage, career, or social situation.

One woman chose a professional way of life and became a top-notch executive in a large Manhattan firm. All during those early years, Viola remained at home with her parents. First, just as she had done in childhood, but eventually she built an extension on the house, so that she had a private apartment. This was not difficult because her father was in the construction business. Most nights of the week, Viola was coming home to mom and dad, and very often to wonderful home-cooked meals. She was happy and contented and not at all aware of being dissatisfied with these arrangements. The great responsibility at work and the mature persona of the executive gave way at home to an often too comfortable childishness.

Then one day Viola found herself trembling as she drove through the Battery Tunnel linking Long Island with New York City's Manhattan. An unfamiliar and acute attack of terror came from nowhere causing her to shake and break out in a cold sweat. That night her anxiety attack was so severe she could not drive home. She left her car in the city and took a taxi home. After two weeks of taxis or friends taking Viola to and from work, she searched for a condominium in the city.

Six months later, Viola was back to driving, delighting in her own place, into interior decorating, choosing her cookware and china in Macy's department store and going out to eat in all the best places in New York City. She started wondering if she should not make a move into another firm, and considered if at forty, it was not too late to ponder some more permanent male relationship and even marriage. Viola had grown up in her twenties and thirties in many ways, but some long-neglected psychological maturing was accomplished when her unconscious psyche took over and demanded the completion of the movement from childhood to adulthood.

The transition from youth to midlife is always a crisis time. In Viola's case, it required the completion of some unfinished business from her earlier adolescent transition. It is a time similar to the crisis of our first birth, and again at the end of childhood. Midlife is a birthing time. But as the child must die to life in the womb to be born, so, too, must the young adult die to life as it was lived in youth, to move into this new birth, the second half of life, a new way of being. The crisis is, will I lose myself in the dying process? Will I refuse to enter into a natural process, leaving life's first half even as I left the womb? Will I suffer the dying and birthing pangs that will bring forth new life?

These words from John's gospel can address this moment in life: "When a woman is in labor, she is sad that her time has come. When she has borne her child, she no longer remembers her pain for joy that a child has been born into the world. In the same way you are sad for a time" (John 16:20-22b). The birth of the Self is what this life juncture is about. Who can believe at first, that the new born baby that they are looking at—that little bundle of wrinkled flesh—will grow to be a beautiful, talented individual? Who could believe at this third birth, that this often deflated, insecure questioner at the juncture to life's second half will become in and through the deflation, insecurity, and questioning a more whole, integrated and open individual?

The work of Ira Progoff in his Journal Workshop Process has been a great influence in helping people to contact their story in a deeply significant way. Speaking of times of developmental crisis in his book, *At a Journal Workshop*, Progoff says:

> Especially misleading is the fact that the active germination of a growth process often takes place at the low seemingly negative phase of a psychological cycle. Thus, at the very time when the most constructive developments are taking place within a person, his [or her] outer appearance may be depressed, confused and even disturbed. Physical growth is easy to recognize, but personal growth is inward and elusive. (18)

One midlife woman had been an entrepreneur with her husband for fifteen years. The founding of a new business had been exciting and she had no time or desire for homemaking. An expensive condominium called for weekly maid service and eating out around business ventures took care of most meals. Suddenly she began to feel edgy. Enthusiasm for new projects was waning. She longed for time off, days off. The nesting instinct had risen unexpectedly in her. Some would say she had been bewitched by the goddess of the hearth, Hera, who was demanding her rightful place in her life.

Recognition came when she started to oversleep and let her husband go off to work alone. Luckily, she was not frightened by this strange new dimension of herself. She welcomed this evolution within herself and took the opportunities she had to let this new part of her have a place in her life. Three years later, in her fiftieth year, she and her husband bought a new home, and she formally became a part-time partner. This woman allowed the evolution of her person to reshape her values and her life-style. By attention to the movements within herself, she found a new dynamism. Indeed, she was on her way to becoming her Self.

The midlife crisis/transition is usually triggered by and centered around an inner or outer event in a person's life. For the woman entre-preneur, it was a whole set of inner feelings that came unbidden. For Rabbi Kushner and his wife, it was an event in their outer life that came uninvited. Rabbi Kushner tells the story in his best-selling book *When Bad Things Happen to Good People*. This is the story of how his son's fatal illness became the catalyst for the evolution of his faith and relationship with God. A dramatic new kind of "growing up" occurred when Kushner realized that he could obey all God's laws, devote himself to doing good, and it would be no guarantee that the good things in life would come his way. Dealing with his son's illness challenged all his youthful beliefs and assumptions. He was forced to reevaluate and redefine his faith in life and his faith in God. He came to realize that God does not want sorrow, pain, death, or evil. God can only help to create a person despite, and in and through the sorrow, death, evil, and pain that comes into some-one's life.

He saw that he himself was free to respond to these events in a way that would foster his collaboration with the work of the Master Potter. He came to realize that all development takes place as one responds to the life events that are molding one. He came to understand also, that there is no guarantee that you will not do evil, even in the midst of striv-ing to be a good person. But even here, the evil you do to yourself and others can eventually be the stuff of bringing about growth and develop-ment, if you contritely and humbly accept responsibility and respond to the reality around you. Life challenges every youthful ideal, belief, and faith itself. Midlife and the mature years call for a maturation of faith on all levels.

In *Pathfinders* Gail Sheehy tells a wonderful story of midlife crisis, transition, and conversion. It is the story of a young forty-year-old manager of the west coast's largest nuclear plant. A prolific scientist, dedicated to progress, he took on being a Cub Scout leader. Slowly, as he conducted his weekly sessions with his own young son and other boys, the openness and beauty of these youngsters began to awaken in him a suspicion and a doubt about the nuclear plant he headed. Other values began to loom large, challenging the work to which he had until then dedicated himself. Eventually, with great risk to his own career, he resigned his position and took on an antinuclear stance that changed him and his lifestyle.

All Growth Comes from the Unconscious

The dynamic process of growth and development inaugurated at the time of conception, continued in our fetal development, infancy, and childhood, continues all throughout the many decades of our adult years and perhaps through the final death process itself. There is not one adulthood. We live through many adulthoods in this long life we have as a gift. Midlife heralds in life's second half with all its possibilities for ongoing development and the evolution of the personality. Developmental psychology and Jung's psychology depict a whole new life with surprising new possibilities for the second half of life as we have already demonstrated.

Whenever retirement comes in a person's midlife or mature years, it always comes as a challenge. It is a major transition time calling for adjustment, ingenuity, creativity, discernment, and soul searching. One couple discerned at retirement time that they would offer to work for a diocese that was economically deprived, as well as in need of creative ministry and personnel. Both found church work to be meaningful personally, and had had success serving as volunteers in a variety of ways in their parish community, as they had moved often around the country. Both were theologically educated. Financially, they were able to donate their services and live on their retirement savings. They took months to search out their new diocese. The day they went off for an interview with a bishop in the southwest, was also the day a prospective buyer for their house signed a contract to buy.

For them, such synchronicity was an obvious affirmation of their decision to sell everything and move to the place that would welcome them into diocesan positions of ministry. Friends, children, and neighbors were amazed at this great risk and their adventurous spirit. Throughout our midlife and mature years, we are invited, again and again, to create and accept opportunities for new beginnings.

When C. G. Jung was asked, "What advice do you give older people?" he answered, "I tell them, live on, live on as though you had centuries and then you will live rightly."

Throughout our long life we are challenged to live life to the fullest. That challenge may be to accept the invitation to just be, to relax, to experience the now. The challenge may be to accept the conflict that arises and use it as an impetus to discover more about the mystery of ourselves. There may be uncharted paths in relationship, and one finds the affective mode becomes for one a new school of learning. We may find that an avenue of knowledge has evaded us and now calls to us for exploration. When Erik Erikson, in his eighties, found himself learning to read Greek so that he could read the Christian scriptures in their original language, he was allowing his religious function to move beyond any state of equilibrium or status quo, into a whole new world of quest. He found food for his Soul. All this is passion for life.

The actor Kirk Douglas, in his midseventies, admitted that he never cultivated a friendship with his children. He did not embrace or hug his boys. Only in his sixties did he begin to change. From then on he served not only as their mentor, especially in the art of acting, but as their friend and warmly and physically showed his affection. Still having the body of a vibrant man, Kirk worked out, maintaining his own strength and vigor, seventy something, while he found many of the unused and dormant parts of his personality becoming sources of new psychic energy. Owning neglected aspects of who he was, Kirk Douglas was creating new paths of deeper significant relationships with others. In his late seventies, Kirk suffered a stroke that affected his speech. But he would not allow the stroke to make him a victim. His vibrant voice and sound was gone, but even with his impaired voice, he went on stage to give a speech and accept a lifetime achievement award. He worked tirelessly with a speech therapist and later on gave an interview on television following the writing of his memoirs. A while later, he was acting again.

Anne Brennan's mother, Ann, reared seven wonderful children. Her mothering style was not very affectionate. She rarely hugged or kissed her children or said words of love and endearment. Besides running the household and caring for her many children, she also helped her husband, Mike, with much of the organization, bookkeeping, etc., of his business. With all this management, she did a terrific job. She was a great thinker and in her youth took things in her stride. She very often reached out to others and opened her home to members of the extended families.

Ann's mature years brought about many changes and one was very welcome by her family. One day the phone rang, and it was Anne's mother. "Anne," she said, "your sister Maureen told me to tell you that I love you." "Mom, what did you say?" Anne asked her mother. Once again, Anne's mother repeated, "Your sister Maureen said to tell you that I love you." Later, Anne found out that she had made a similar call to each of her midlife children. That was the beginning of a whole new way of life for that eighty-year-old. Always caring, but never too affectionate in word or deed, Anne's mother never again let an opportunity go by without telling one of her children that indeed, "she loved them." Of course, they thought she loved them. But this newly awakened, affectionate side of Ann Brennan, Senior, transformed her and her relationships with each child of hers. The transformation affected all her relationships with other family members and friends, as well.

So often at a Long Life Directions Program, we say, "It is a false myth that you cannot teach an old dog a new trick." "Repeat after me," one of us will jokingly say, "You *can* teach an old dog a new trick." With Anne's mother, she covered over embarrassment at "such a foolish thing," as saying "I love you," by using her daughter as an excuse. "Maureen said I should." But once the ice was broken, her affectionate side demanded opportunities for these loving exchanges.

Thomas Jefferson and John Adams had much in common. Both played crucial roles in the early history of our nation. Both men gave birth to our early documents: The Declaration of Independence written by Jefferson, as well as The Articles of Confederation and The Constitution of the United States of America. Both men served the country abroad in France and both occupied the highest office in the nation, the presidency.

On New Year's Day in 1812, John Adams wrote to Thomas Jefferson, breaking an eleven-year silence and a long period of enmity that had grown between them. When this long estrangement came to an end, Adams was seventy-six and Jefferson seventy-eight. That New Year's letter began a long period of letter writing and provided the two men with an intimacy that helped to cradle their old age. One hundred fifty-three letters passed between them (104 from Adams and 49 from Jefferson). In 1816, Adams wrote to Jefferson, "You and I ought not to die before we have explained ourselves to each other." Both men wanted to live to celebrate the fiftieth anniversary of the Declaration of Independence. They lived to celebrate July 4, 1826, the fiftieth anniversary and *both* men died on *that* very day.

> If ever two men in history chose and controlled the moment of their dying, they were John Adams and Thomas Jefferson. Each was determined to reach the 50th anniversary of the signing of the Declaration of Independence and neither knew that their gentle competition for this great milepost would end in victory and in death for both of them. (Brodie, 633)

Thomas Jefferson died earlier in the day and word had not reached the Adams house. When John Adams died, he breathed his last words, "Thomas Jefferson still lives."

New Year's Day is always a time for resolutions, for turning toward becoming all we are called to be, our better selves. January 1, 1812, was a blessed day for Adams and Jefferson. The ending of their silence and warfare marked a change in personality and developed into an opportunity rich in rewards of challenges and comfort. There is no substitute for companionship, the most blessed of graces. Our personalities are not unchangeably set. We can change, grow, and develop at any time, and at any age. In our mature years, we can always mellow. Conversion is no stranger to the later years.

The Conversion of Oscar Schindler and Zaccheus in the Gospel of Luke

The midlife and mature years are the years for the most profound psychological and spiritual growth. These are the years for separating oneself from the herd, even while moving toward greater solidarity and universality. Separation from the herd calls for facing up to your own personal negative shadow and to the collective shadow. The power of the shadow is exemplified remarkably in the story of Oscar Schindler in the book and Oscar-winning film, *Schindler's List*. Oscar Schindler had developed into an opportunist and profiteer. He, a nominal Christian, takes advantage of the Jews and the Nazi situation in Europe. Without a twinge of conscience, he moves into the homes vacated by the Jews as they are by force moved into ghettoes and eventually work camps and death camps. Leaving behind their properties and life savings, Schindler, a sophisticated scavenger and opportunist, makes his fortune.

A shrewd businessman and excellent "at presentation," Schindler operates factories and employs the Jews. The Nazis want production to continue on all levels to support the war effort, and so, the Jews are allowed to work for him, for no pay, except salvation from the death camps. He shares his profit with no one.

In the film, there is a magnificent scene where Liam Neeson, playing Oscar Schindler, and Ben Kingsley (who played Gandhi in another famous film), his overseer, have an exchange. The overseer brings an old Jewish man to him, one who has been begging for the opportunity to express his gratitude to Schindler, personally. He is so grateful for the work that has saved him and his family from deportation. In that moving scene, gratitude, praise, and thanks pour forth from the old man's heart. Schindler is appalled at the words of thanks and praise. He begins to see himself as he really is. He is coming to consciousness. He knows in a new way what it means to be using this man and the others for his own gain.

In another scene, we observe Schindler beginning to see not just himself but the Jews. He dares to kiss a young Jewish child gratefully, who gives him a birthday gift, in front of the Nazi soldiers. Schindler, in this act, both steps out of the herd, and moves toward solidarity with the Jews. He begins to see the Jew as human, as person, as himself. The Nazis in the scene see the Jews as nonhuman, as animal. "Who would kiss a dog or a pig?" Oscar, on the other hand, kisses a human girl child.

As we watch the film, we witness the moral and spiritual awakening of Oscar Schindler. He rises to spiritual heights risking his own life to save hundreds of Jews by employing more and more Jews in his factories, now, not for gain but for the preservation of his brothers and sisters. He becomes "as cunning as serpents and yet harmless as doves" (Matthew 10:16b) and not for his own gain but for the Kingdom of God.

The conversion of Schindler from opportunist and profiteer to humanitarian was the most profound soul-making. His experience of solidarity with the Jews was a deep religious experience. It took him out of the herd and resonated in the moral fibres of his being. The moral and spiritual resources that he had repressed within himself came into play, and he touched others in a most heroic and unique way.

A Jungian viewpoint can give a great understanding of Schindler's conversion from opportunist and profiteer to humanitarian. Yes, it was grace, but we can understand the psychic dimensions. His ego had been characterized by opportunist and profiteer. That is what he had consciously made of himself. Buried within his unconscious were the opposing virtues which he denied: humanitarian, hero, and savior. Very often the shadow, with any one of us, is some neglected positive power, value or virtue. As Oscar's shadow, in opposition to profiteer and opportunist, became creative forces demanding to be active, the Self brought about a creative marriage. In changing to the humanitarian, all the creative energy, shrewdness, smarts, cunning that Oscar had formerly used in being a profiteer and opportunist, was redirected and used to fulfill his new task and vocation, saving the Jews.

Here we are reminded of a similar story in the New Testament in the Gospel of Luke 19:1–10. Jesus enters Jericho and while passing through the city, Zaccheus, being small of stature, climbs a tree in an effort to see the Nazarene. The gospel says "He was the chief tax collector and a wealthy man." For the Jew, Zaccheus, to be a chief tax collector meant that Zaccheus collected the taxes for Rome from his own Jewish people. To be a wealthy tax collector meant that Zaccheus had succumbed to being an opportunist and a profiteer. He charged the people, as was the custom, higher taxes than Rome demanded and pocketed the difference for himself. The Roman officials always looked the other way. They were only concerned that the tax collector got the taxes from the people, and had the correct amount for the Roman government. If the tax collector made something for himself on the side, it did not concern them. Zaccheus's wealth was all made dishonestly, and the result of the increased financial burden that he unjustly placed upon his own people.

When Jesus arrives and Zaccheus is anxious to see him, he is already opening himself to change. Symbolically he is opening himself unconsciously to the other side of his own personality. The Nazarene has a reputation for being someone who does not follow the herd. Zaccheus knows that he is someone who stands with and for the masses. Jesus represents his better side, his greater Self. Zaccheus, in his youth, had taken a different path than the one Jesus embarked upon. His interest in Jesus implied a question about his own ego development and his own way of life.

When Jesus came to the sycamore tree, he stopped, looked up and saw Zaccheus, and he must have taken a long knowing and loving look. He said, "Zaccheus, hurry down. I mean to stay at your house today" (Luke 19:5). Jesus did not spurn Zaccheus. He sees in this opportunist and profiteer the possibilities of a great man and a true humanitarian. His invitation to dine with him, to enter his home, was an invitation to change and transformation. Zaccheus welcomes Jesus with excitement and delight. The ego and Self encounter one another with recognition and mutual respect. Accepting the invitation, Zaccheus says, "I give half my belongings, Lord, to the poor. If I have defrauded anyone in the least, I pay him or her back fourfold" (Luke 19:8). Jesus understands the true significance of the words of Zaccheus and proclaims their meaning, "Today salvation has come to this house, for this is what it means to be a child of Abraham. The Son of Man has come to search out and save what was lost" (Luke 19:9–10).

All the ingenuity and shrewdness that Zaccheus had used to become a wealthy man is now turned into caring for the poor and making reparation to those whom he had defrauded. Zaccheus's shadow interacts with his own ego and the Self in him becomes a greater reality. The Self, in the name of Jesus, orchestrated this great conversion. The Self has a remarkable way of not despising the less than lovely in us. Jesus did not despise Zaccheus and He did not despise the opportunist in him. Instead, he thought, "How can I redirect this energy for good purposes?" The Self can incorporate everything into the new creation that we are each becoming.

The Gold in the Shadow

What shadow aspects of your personality can be for you a source of enrichment, change, conversion, transformation? You never lose or totally integrate your shadow as long as you live. The shadow represents all the unlived aspects of yourself. It is the unconscious, unknown part of yourself. So often we find the shadow reflected in our conflicts, emotions, projections. Zaccheus had admired Jesus. He was projecting onto Jesus his own ability to be for others, as Jesus was. To be intimate with Jesus, he had to withdraw that projection and live out this other side of himself. He could not be satisfied with letting Jesus carry his shadow.

One woman wrote letters to the editor of the town newspaper condemning a topless bar that had opened in the downtown area. She had never written to an editor before this experience. Next, she called her church and suggested that the pastor speak at the monthly clergy meeting about this situation and organize a combined church protest for the new establishment. Her family found she was becoming obsessed with the whole thing and all conversation was about the decline of the neighborhood. Her own grown sons were in fear that she would discover they had made a visit once, just out of curiosity.

Then, another woman's letter appeared in the same paper and it had an enormous effect on the woman protester. The second woman was also disappointed about the location of the topless bar, but she was more concerned with the *violent* outrage that so many of the citizens were expressing. In one short sentence she expressed her fear that "the women most outraged were flat-chested women who had not been greatly endowed." She suggested that women who had been dissatisfied with their own figure and shapeliness were usually the same people to be violently adamant in rejecting something like a topless bar or something as simple as a bikini on a beach. That had been her own experience as a young woman when bikinis first became fashionable. From that day on, and because of that letter to the editor, this woman protester began to let go the violence of her opposition. Indeed, she had always been, much to her sorrow, flat-chested. This reminds us of a story from ancient Japanese culture. If a warrior found that he had hatred in his heart for the enemy, he had to lay down his weapons and depart. He could not continue to fight until he had his own house in order.

At another time, a religious sister was missioned in another country involved in a deep political and conflictual situation. After working there for close to a decade, she petitioned her congregation and the church in the area to allow her to establish a small house of reconciliation. The sole purpose for the new establishment was to be dedicated to nonviolence, prayer, and work toward reconciling the opposing political, racial, and religious forces that were at war with one another. Her proposal was accepted, a house was found, and plans were being made for who would join her as a core group.

At this time, the nun had a dream. In her dream, at night, she entered the bedroom of another sister and clubbed her to death. This very short dream initially shocked and terrified the sister. "What could it mean?" she asked. After much reflection, soul searching, and prayer, as well as some dream work, she came to see that her dream was about her shadow side. It was telling her, "Yes, your ego or conscious self is dedicated to nonviolence and reconciliation. You are so formed in these virtues that you have the audacity to think that you can bring these warring groups together. Do you know, are you aware, that within you is a very violent warrior?" All the scriptures of the great world religions offer counsel on the need of humility and the danger of judging others. All call us to see and hear and understand with new eyes, ears, and insight. "Why look at the speck in your brother's or sister's eye when you miss the plank in your own. How can you say to your brother or sister, 'Let me remove the speck from your eye, yet fail yourself to see the plank lodged in your own?' Hypocrite, remove the plank from your own eye first; then you will see clearly enough to remove the speck from your brother's or sister's eye" (Luke 6:41–42).

Unlike the woman with the topless bar, this woman did not abandon her project. She understood her dream as an education so that she would have the major requirements necessary for making her project a success. The sister had to own her own violence and not project it upon either of the warring parties. She had to know her own propensity for evil and not see herself as so different from the people she hoped to serve so lovingly. The sister's dream was a warning, an education and a message from the Self. Indeed, it became a turning point in her life both personally and professionally. Throughout our midlife and later years, we are challenged with welcomed and nonwelcomed manifestations of the other side of the personality. All such shadow experiences are gifts from the unconscious and with proper interaction are means of growth and development.

A nun in her late eighties went to her congregation's retirement house and found herself quite despondent. This was very uncharacteristic of her. She had begun to lose her eyesight and her hearing. With good Irish humor she said, "The people around her thought I had lost a lot more than that." When a friend pointed out to her that she seemed to be close to despair, she was quite stunned. The word *despair* for her was like shock treatment. "Girl," she said to herself, "get a hold on yourself."

For months, the sister was not able to pray. If she went to chapel, she could not hear the readings or the preaching. She could not read the prayers or hymns. When she went to meditate, all she experienced was an empty weariness. Her usual ways of praying and a devotional life of more than eighty years appeared to be shipwrecked. She was in a "dark night of the soul." When lovingly confronted with her "near despair," the old nun went to meditation and the memories of her early childhood in Ireland flooded her mind. "I saw myself," she told us, "rolling down the hills of Ireland. I began to recite all the little poems and prayers I learned as a child. And from that day on, I have had the best meditations, the prayer of my life."

So often when your psyche finds itself in shallow ground, it seeks nurturance in the depths of the unconscious. The old nun knew nothing about Jungian psychology. She was unfamiliar with the term "unconscious," but her unconscious came to her aid and introduced her to a whole new way of praying in her late eighties and nineties. Her prayer life had become dry and routine. Her failing eyesight and loss of hearing put her at the mercy of inner resources that she did not know she had. They prepared her for a gift from her inner sea. Our unconscious is a sea of new creative life to embellish our later years.

The archetypal Child, with all her powers of imagination and fantasy, introduced this woman to a new way of praying. "A little child shall lead them," the scriptures tutor us (Isaiah 9:6). The archetypal Child in each of us is part of the collective unconscious. The inner Child is the psychic power and potential to be like a child: open to the new, adventurous, hopeful, playful, energetic; open to the imagination and fantasy, etc. These are all wonderful qualities that can come alive in us in our later years. We can call upon our archetypal Child to bring new life to us and to use our great powers of imagination and fantasy as the old nun did. If the Child has not been alive in us, he or she can be found in the depths of our shadow and unconscious self and can be resurrected.

Trials are no respector of age. But age can give us the endurance and resiliency to face up to great challenges. The resources are within. Endurance makes for great souls. Florida Scoot-Maxwell ruminates on age in her notebook:

> Age puzzles me. I thought it was a quiet time. My seventies were interesting, and fairly serene, but my eighties are passionate. I grow more intense as I age. To my own surprise, I burst out with hot conviction. Only a few years ago, I enjoyed my tranquility; now I am so disturbed by the outer world and by human quality in general that I want to put things right, as though I still owed a debt to life. I must calm down. I am far too frail to indulge in moral fervor. (13–14)

How wonderful to see this change in Florida, from her seventies to her eighties. How wonderful to witness the surge of energy, the fruit of her Soul, the activity of her Spirit; no less powerful though encased in a frail and elderly body. How wonderful to see her passion for life. We must each hold on to what it is we are passionate about. There is life in abundance. We need to reverence our unconscious in all its manifestations. We need to reverence our shadow side, as the seeds of new growth and new beginnings; to accept the invitation to "grow old along with me!" and to "see all and be not afraid." We are called to drink fully of the cup of our long lives. For those who do so, like Jesus, each will be able to say, "No one, after drinking old wine, wants new. He or she says, 'I find the old wine better' " (Luke 5:38).

One Story, One Life:
Past, Present, and Future

Secrets

Y ou can never know when in your adult life you will be asked to enter into a reconciliation with dimensions of your own story or the story of people you love. You can be sure it will happen again and again throughout the second half of your life. Something inside you begins to make itself known and you are called upon to bring to consciousness aspects of your story that are repressed. One woman, Janet, had ill feelings toward her maternal grandmother and her mother all her life. It was only after her mother's death that the ill feelings began to simmer within her, causing great emotional pain. The normal process of grieving a parent's death was not possible. Janet could not grieve her mother's death because she was still grieving the fact that she never had affective feelings for her mother. She was grieving the fact that her own mother never seemed to own her daughter. She had no sense of being known, loved, appreciated, wanted, or cherished by her mother. It was something she had always felt but never verbalized.

When a child, Janet, her parents, and her two older brothers, lived in her grandmother's large house. The child could not express her feelings regarding the suffocating atmosphere in the house. Looking back as an adult, she used the words, "hostile and chilling" to talk about her early life in grandma's house. But even as she used these words she had the big questions, Why? Why was it this way? Underneath the question was the deeper unconscious question: is there something wrong with me? Janet became a productive woman. Her beautiful quiet presence and gentle charm made other people really like her. But she never married and never came to a genuine sense of self-acceptance. As her parents aged and her mother, in her eighties, found it difficult to care for her own home, Janet's parents came to live with her. For five years, Janet had tried to do and be for her parents. But the ill feelings toward her mother never changed.

One day, nine months after her mother's death, Janet, no longer able to contain her pain, shared her distress with her eighty-year-old father. "Did you love mother?" she asked her father. Janet's father affirmed his love for his wife and spoke openly and honestly about her. Then Janet shared her great secret. "I never felt that mother loved me. I never even thought she knew who I was. It was like she didn't see me. I could have been any other baby, any other girl or woman, and it wouldn't have mattered to mother. I felt this way as a child. I felt this way the past five years with you and mother living here with me. Daddy, didn't you ever notice this? Why was it this way? Is there something wrong with me?" Then, Janet went on to talk about her early childhood and life with grandma. She used the words "hostile and chilling." At that, the old man, who loved his daughter dearly, went and took his weeping child in his arms and comforted her. He was always reserved, composed, and emotionally constrained, but he stepped out of character to meet this crisis. Janet's father expressed his deep sorrow that he had not known about her feelings for the last fifty-five years, the length of her life. He then wept himself before he told Janet that perhaps he knew what caused her profound sense of rejection.

Janet did not despise or hate her mother. She just felt the overwhelming pain of not being accepted, known, and loved. She listened to the story of her mother's dismay many years ago to find that she was with child again. Her two sons were only three and two, and she had not wanted any more children, at least not then. Her father came home one day to find her mother in bed, and her grandmother almost frantic. Her grandmother had tried to abort the child, but had failed. Her mother was bleeding, in great pain, and emotionally and physically exhausted. Aware of his wife's distress, he gave her all the care, affection, love, and attention that he could give. Feeling guilty and responsible, he never relented on giving his wife that same loving attention to all her needs, all her life. Janet's mother came to accept her pregnancy, but never came really to see, love, accept, and cherish the charming baby girl that entered her life. For fifty-five years, Janet, consciously and unconsciously, was the invader.

Janet's father's words poured out upon her broken and bleeding heart, like a soothing medicine. The story of her grandmother's reaching in to sever her life from her mother's womb came to her heart and her ears as though she had known it all her life. To understand the hostility she had felt as a child and know the why of it, after so many years, was a deep comfort. She could deal with the story. She could deal with the knowing. Janet could not deal with the unanswered question, Why? Eventually, Janet was able to make her peace with her deceased mother. She was grateful she had given her life. She knew intellectually that her mother did love her. Freed of the guilt herself, of not feeling love or affection for her mother, Janet went on accepting and loving herself and reaching out to others. The pain is there, but it no longer dominates her life. A new open relationship has developed between father and daughter, both comforting and challenging each of them at this juncture in their lives.

This story demonstrates in a remarkable way how someone's personal unconscious story can be unknowingly active in their conscious life. When Janet heard the secret, she had an intuitive sense that she had known it all along. As we move through the second half of life and into our mature years, there is a need to know our own true story at greater depth. We do not all have a terrible secret to bring to consciousness, but the fragments of our story are the precious pieces of who we are today. We are each fashioned by history. Janet's pain made her reach out to her father for an answer. She was fortunate to have a father who could tell her the story of her unborn life.

A Call to Remember

Sometimes we must live in mystery. But more often through reflection, journaling, conversation, and storytelling we can gather together the chapters of our lives. We can go back to the places of our history to gather the story together. We were traveling in Hawaii when Honolulu was flooded with seventy- and eighty-year-old men and women. They had returned to the scene of Pearl Harbor on the fiftieth anniversary of Japan's infamous bombing. Those events were part of the very psyche of the people who came back to re-member. A month earlier, we had been giving workshops in Singapore and Malaysia. At the time of World War II they were English colonies. The Japanese invaded and occupied the two countries for the duration of the war. Most of the participants in our programs had been infants and children during the occupation. Some had no schooling until they were ten or eleven because of the Japanese occupation. These people were looking back to this unfortunate childhood to understand themselves and gain insights about themselves. Acceptance, forgiveness, and healing create in us an affirmation of the story that is uniquely ours. Jung says, "Each person has a story. Derangement comes when the story is denied or rejected. Rediscovery of the story is the cure."

One seventy-year-old man was confronted with a man in his sixties who had defrauded him forty years earlier while in his employment. The encounter was an unexpected meeting at the doors of a church. As the men recognized one another, the thief confessed in tears. The seventy-year-old embraced him and said, "It's over now. It's all right. Gone and forgotten. Be at peace." What an opportunity for both men! A moment of grace. A triumph for each man's greater Self. We each have within us the inner resources for coming to a genuine integrity regarding our past, present, and future. Opportunities will present themselves and we must grasp them.

A sixty-year-old woman discovered on her mother's death bed that she had been adopted and where she could find the papers on her adoption. The mother of five children herself, she had often regretted not having any brothers or sisters of her own. Her husband and children encouraged her to search out her birth mother. When she did, she found a lonely woman who had never married.

Her mother was only sixteen when she gave birth to her. She gave her up for adoption because she wanted to finish school, and she had no way of supporting her baby. She had gone on to be a teacher and had just recently retired. This woman's story came knocking on her door when her sixty-year-old daughter arrived at her front door looking for her birth mother. Not all stories would have this happy ending. But happy or not, the time often comes when we are asked to own our stories in remarkable ways.

Today, that woman has come to know her daughter, son-in-law, and grandchildren. Deprived for years of being a mother, she now has a built-in family. She had, within her as a sixteen-year-old, the resources to accept life and creatively handle her situation. A good principal and compassionate, understanding teachers were her main support.

Today, as an older woman, she has again the resources within herself to respond to a new invitation to life.

What will come knocking on your door from within or without? Will you reach down to your own depths, touch your own Soul and express that Soul in the life choices you make at sixty, seventy, eighty, and again at ninety?

A ninety-year-old woman shared a secret with us. It was as though our presentation on the unconscious and its manifestations in our lives freed her up to speak about something that had happened seventy-two years earlier. As a young woman in eastern Europe, she had entered religious life. She had an older sister in the same congregation, living and working in Rome, Italy. The congregation was sending thirty sisters to America and Sister Johanna was hoping to be one of the chosen ones. The day came when the thirty sisters were told who they were, and told to prepare to go to the office of emigration to get the necessary papers, etc.

Johanna was not one of the chosen ones, and she was greatly disappointed that she was not going to America. One night soon after she had a dream. In her dream, her older sister, the nun in Rome, was dressed in a beautiful white gown, like a bride. Johanna looked at her lovely sister with delight and admiration. As she did so, her sister began to rise off the ground and go off into the skies or heavens. Knowing what was happening, Johanna cried out, "Please don't go. If you must go, come back and take me with you." Johanna's sister smiled and said, "No, no, Johanna. You must stay. You are going to go to America to do God's work."

Sister Johanna was puzzled by her dream. What could it mean? Two weeks later, word came from Rome that Sister Johanna's sister had taken ill and died. She died the very night that Johanna had her dream. When the sisters went for their papers, one failed a literacy test and the congregation picked another sister to make up the thirty. It was Sister Johanna.

All her life, Sister Johanna knew without a doubt that coming to America was indeed her destiny. It was for her "the will of God." It was her fate. It was meant to be. But she never shared her dream or vision with anyone. There was no climate to accept the bizarre, the unusual, the synchronistic event, the unexplainable, the miraculous. As we talked about the unconscious, giving some examples of synchronicity, Sister Johanna found words to put upon her unique experience in the form of a most unusual dream. It was with relief and joy that she told her story of seventy years ago, as though it were yesterday.

Once again, Sister Johanna knew, "You are not alone. No one is alone." In her mature years, she was secure in her destiny. She was her story.

The Story Continues

In Joan and Erik Erikson's theory of the eight stages of life, the last stage of life is described as the confrontation between integrity and despair. It demands a strong sense of integrity for who we have been, for who we are, and who we are becoming. Jung tells us that if our "story is denied or rejected by ourselves, derangement comes." The only way we can be cured is, "to rediscover the story." We must know ourselves in the hands of the Beloved. The sense of Self must be strong in us. If not, we will succumb to despair as we begin to experience some of the terrible losses often experienced in the aging process.

It appears at times that our body becomes our enemy and attacker. It can hold us back from the many things we long to do. It disrupts our plans and schedules. We look at ourselves in the mirror and do not recognize ourselves. Our body is the precious garment we were each clothed in at birth. How can we adopt a loving and grateful attitude toward this loyal friend, partners through life? A strong sense of Self, our own Soul and an intense feeling for the journey we are on allows us to transcend the echoes of decline and pursue the spiritual call for transformation.

We had an eighty-year-old woman make a four-hour drive to come to one of our Mid-Life Directions Workshops for people 35-to-65-plus. We had an intense weekend schedule beginning with a session Friday evening and closing after lunch on Sunday. When the workshop is fit into a weekend, it is very full, allowing little free time. Saturday afternoon followed a very full morning. The eighty-year-old came up and said to us, "I love what you are doing, Dearies, but if I don't have twenty minutes of shut-eye, I won't be able to go on. You don't mind, do you?" We assured her that we did not mind and told her to do whatever she must to regain her vitality. We both thought she was going to leave the gathering room and go to her room for a while or even for the rest of the afternoon. But to our great surprise and delight, she went over to one side of the meeting room where there were a few lounge chairs, tables, and couches. She spread her eighty-something frame flat out on one of the couches for twenty minutes. After which, she got up, took a cup of coffee from one of the tables and rejoined the group listening to a presentation.

This eighty-year-old was liberated from established conventions. To this day, we are both delighted by the memory of that woman. She modeled healthy aging for both of us, and for the group that was mostly made up of forty- and fifty-year-olds and a few sixty- and seventy-year-olds. How comfortable she was with herself. How well she knew herself. She knew her limitations. She did the long four-hour drive from her home to the workshop location. She accepted that challenge. She did not stay home because the program's tight schedule would be too taxing for her. Perhaps ten or fifteen years ago it would not have been at all taxing. She would do what she could do and make whatever adjustments needed to be made. She was not at all self-conscious. She did not shy away with, "What will people think if I take a catnap right here on the couch in everyone's presence?" We are sure half the room wished at that time to do exactly the same as she did. Even to think of it brings a big smile to our faces. Not in a condescending way but with delight, admiration, and a healthy envy. Will we ever become that free?

This very same woman shared with us on Sunday morning that she had come to a new level in understanding some of the past events in her life that clustered around her fiftieth year, during her reflections and journaling on the weekend. She had carried much pain, anger, and resentment toward some people for the past thirty years, but felt that she had received the grace not only to forgive and to let go but to understand that so much of her own maturation in the past thirty years came about because of the action she took as a result of that conflictual situation. The life changes she made at that time were choices for personal integrity, growth, and individuation. The very situation and people that had hurt her also caused her to choose life and growth and forced her to take a different path.

Here was a woman in her mature years, having matured so much, still growing. The past is all within each of us, and we need to reclaim it. We ponder questions about events of our own story. What caused this to happen? What were the results? What was the significance? This is an open-book test and leads us to refind ourselves by reclaiming the past but not by mere reminiscence but a reinterpretation and a reintegration, a re-member-ing of our own true selves. This woman seized the opportunity the workshop presented her with to directly enter into her re-member-ing, her own Soul making.

He not busy being born is busy dying. (Bob Dylan)

Again and again throughout our midlife years and throughout our mature years, we are called on to become new. We are given opportunities for new birth, new blossoming. Our soul leaps up, transcending the mundane, transcending the pain and defeats of life, and we are, as it were, remade. From out of nowhere, revelations come from the hidden depths of the psyche. We are both confronted and comforted. The life-giving waters within bring forth new life. We are astonished as we gain access to the inner sources of psychic life. Our whole life takes on new meaning and the life of the soul is intensified. There are opportunities to:

renew	return	revision
refound	rejuvenate	reinterpret
recollect	remake	repattern
rebirth	reform	reinvent
reenergize	retune	refashion
redevelop	readjust	remember

When Jesus encountered the Samaritan woman in the Gospel of John, He tells her that He can give her "living water." "Whoever drinks the water I give her will never be thirsty; no, the water I give shall become a fountain within her, leaping up to provide eternal life." (John 4:14) Christ is the Archetype of the Self, Jung tells us. Each one of us can look for and expect a release of the living waters within our own psyche and soul to refresh us, and release the seeds of growth and transformation. This inner fountain is the birthing waters. Christ, God, the Greater Self the image of God that I am, calls each of us to this fountain within. Only poetry can capture these spiritual realities and make them expressible. Jesus was a poet when He spoke of the "fountain leaping up to provide eternal life."

At another time, speaking to Nicodemus, Jesus said "that no one can see the Kingdom of God unless he or she is born again." Nicodemus, unable to grasp the spiritual reality Jesus was talking about, questioned Jesus: "How can a grown man be born again? He certainly cannot enter his mother's womb and be born a second time!" But Jesus replied, "No one can enter the Kingdom of God unless s/he is born of water and the Spirit. A person is born physically of human parents, but s/he is born spiritually of the Spirit. Do not be surprised when I tell you that you must be born again." (John 3:3–7) The human person has the spiritual capacity for rebirth. Not once, not just "twice born," but again and again in this long life. This is our birthright, and we must claim it.

Love and Forgiveness

We each need to give honor to the chapters of our lives. The ones of which we are proud or not proud need to be owned and understood anew. God did not expect any one of us not to make mistakes, not ever to fail, never to be imperfect. Yet life wants us to experience fully the person we are becoming, in, through, and beyond the disappointment we have been, at times, to others and to ourselves.

Mohandas K. Gandhi knew that forgiveness was at the heart of sanity. If we are each related, one to another, then harmony with others is essential to personal harmony and our personal welfare. It is necessary for us to come to a sense of solidarity with others. Earlier, we mentioned Schindler coming to a sense of solidarity with the Jews. This solidarity is a felt sense of the hidden reality of our common bonds, our common destiny and interrelatedness. Gandhi knew that solidarity was at the heart of individual salvation and the salvation of a nation. Today, we would add the salvation of the universe. In his story and in the award winning film, *Gandhi*, there is a scene that brilliantly and simply exemplifies the solidarity he called for, taught, and lived himself.

Gandhi called for nonviolence. Many of the differing factions protesting and demonstrating together were, in reality, bitter enemies themselves, and they despised each other. This contempt for each other led to internal wars. A distraught man, on the verge of insanity because of grief, came to Gandhi for help. He was in need of deliverance. He had lost his son, murdered by the reviled and despised enemy. Gandhi told him that if he wanted his health, sanity, and peace of mind he must go and find a boy the same age as his own dead son, an orphan boy of the despised enemy group. He must love that boy and rear that boy as his very own son. He was called to step outside the herd. He was called to a radical change of attitude. He was invited to reach down to other unknown levels in his own heart. In rearing this boy as his own son, he must also rear him, connected to his roots, as a member of the despised fraction.

Purging himself, or allowing himself to be purged of all deadly anger and resentment, would bring about a restoration of his person. In losing his son he had lost a vital part of himself. By owning to a common humanity and claiming a boy of the hated fraction as his own son, his own flesh and blood, he was opening himself to solidarity with the enemy. He would find his own soul when he came to the realization that we are all part of one great soul. We are all God's creation. This was a call to maturation. A mature adult is open to transformation. A mature adult deals successfully with the demands to grow, develop, and change throughout life.

Gandhi pointed the way to this crazed and tortured mourner. He found a way for this man to claim his story, the events of his life in the past (his son's death by the enemy's action) and his present (the insanity caused by both grief and hatred). He was beside himself. He no longer possessed himself. He was possessed by grief and hatred. Only self-transcendence, pure unrestrained love could release him. He was given the invitation to leap into individuation. On the outside the call came from Mohandas Gandhi. On the inside the call came from the Self, from the innate Wisdom buried deep within him and in each of us. Going to Gandhi in his pain, he was projecting the Self and his own Wisdom on this charismatic leader. If Gandhi's words resonate within him, he can reclaim the Self by withdrawing the projection and doing the heroic and unthinkable. He can take a boy into his own heart and home and still rear him as a member of the despised faction. At this point, his story takes a dramatic shift in course. He takes on a new attitude. Only love has enough fire to burn away the anger and hatred.

Each of us has a Gandhi within our own depths. To this old wise man and old wise woman within, we must turn with the life's hurts and wounds that tear us apart or numb us into zombies like the little crippled boy in *The Secret Garden* or the heart of Scrooge in the Christmas classic. In a sense, Gandhi represented the inner father within each of us. This inner Archetypal Father can confront us, can challenge us to be all that we can be. We must learn to reach in and allow the inner Father to father us. We also have an inner Archetypal Mother as part of our psychic equipment. Often in our midlife and later years, this inner Mother will console us and comfort us. We are not alone. The richness within is a treasure that wants to be found and wants to participate in our life. Conflicts, pain, and defeats make us vulnerable and open to the Kingdom of God within.

The famous writer, C. S. Lewis tells us, "We must forgive all our enemies or be damned." Nevertheless, the struggles to forgive ourselves and to forgive others is a battle each of us must fight. All the great world religions speak of the necessity of love and the necessity of forgiveness. We humans are made with the capacity to love ourselves and to love others. We have the inbuilt spiritual capacity to forgive ourselves and to forgive others. To forgive means to give up resentment and the claim to requital on account of an offense. The classic story of forgiveness is the "Prodigal Son" or "Forgiving Father" told by Jesus and found in Luke's Gospel (Luke 15:11–32). We know Christ, speaking of his own murderers, said, "Father, forgive them; they do not know what they are doing" (Luke 23:34). Jesus set no limit on the extent of our forgiveness. When Peter asked Jesus, "Lord, how often must I forgive my brother if he wrongs me? As often as seven times?" Jesus answered, "Not seven, I tell you, but seventy times seven times" (Matthew 18:21–22). Again, Jesus said, "If your brother does something wrong, reprove him, and if he is sorry, forgive him. And if he wrongs you seven times a day and seven times comes back to you and says, 'I am sorry,' you must forgive" (Luke 16:4).

The celebrated Christian writer, Marcus Borg, tells us that his study of other religions has made him a nonexclusivist Christian. He saw that both Jesus and Buddha introduced people to a new way of being and seeing. Both taught a path of transformation that was both spiritual and psychological. Six centuries before Jesus, Buddha was calling people to live the life of the spirit. He gave people a map on how to conduct their lives, how to travel on the journey of life and how to free their hearts and be in peace. Both Jesus and Buddha, Borg tells us, provided identical advice on loving, forgiving, living a full life, and experiencing the sacred. Borg's wonderful little book, *Jesus and Buddha: The Parallel Savings*, makes a beautiful meditation book for anyone seeking a spiritual life.

Do to others as you would have them do to you. (Luke 6:31)

Consider others as yourself. (DHAMMAPADA, 10.1)

Love your enemies, do good to those who hate you, bless those who curse you, pray for those who abuse you. From anyone who takes away your coat do not withhold even your shirt. Give to everyone who begs from you; and if anyone takes away your goods, do not ask for them again (Luke 6:27–30).

Hatreds do not ever cease in this world by hating, but by love; overcome evil by good. Overcome the miser by giving, overcome the liar by truth. (DHAMMAPADA 1:5 & 17.3)

This is my commandment, that you love one another as I have loved you. No one has greater love than this, to lay down one's life for one's friends (John 15:12–13).

Just as a mother would protect her only child at the risk of her own life, even so, cultivate a boundless heart toward all beings. Let your thoughts of boundless love pervade the whole world (SUTTA NI-PATA, 149–50).

Take Down the Love Letters

It is in midlife and again in old age that we can look back at our own history (his story and her story) and like an historian gain a new, more genuine and wholistic perspective of the days of our lives. Like a historian, we can come to see the facts and dates, the stepping stones, the decisions, the unexpected events, the triumphs, the decisions, the influences, the significant people, the defeats and failures, the evil done by us, and the evil done against us, the paths and dreams and visions that make up the journey, the Soul making that is each of us.

A favorite question on a history test is: "What is the significance of . . . ?" And another is: "What caused . . . ?" Another questions is: "What were the results of . . . ?" Age gives us a perspective to re-evaluate, re-interpret, re-found, re-claim, re-member our own story. That story is the story of the ego and the Self as one. We need to re-member our story. That is, we need to put it together and become aware of who we have become in the years of our living. Nothing is wasted. All is gathered together. We see the ego being formed in childhood and youth. We sense the Self engineering our life's work, our call, our uniqueness. We come to see that even our mistakes were mysteriously worked into the process of our own becoming more whole. We come to understand that life has been generating our soul. We sense and experience the Self in ourselves. Times of recollection allow us to recollect the fragments of our story.

LOVE AFTER LOVE

The Time will come
when, with elation,
you will greet yourself arriving
at your own door, in your own mirror,
and each will smile at the other's welcome.
and say, sit here. Eat.

You will love the stranger who was yourself.
Give wine. Give bread. Give back your heart
to itself, to the stranger who has loved you.

All your life, whom you ignored
for another, who knows you by heart.
Take down the love letters from the bookshelf,

the photographs, the desperate notes,
peel your own image from the mirror.
Sit. Feast on your life.

> Derek Walcott,
> Nobel Prize Laureate for Literature,
> *Sea Grapes*

The Psalms proclaim this consciousness: "You knit me in my mother's womb" (Psalm 139:13). We come from the heavens. We are knitted by God—in our mother's womb, in our childhood, in young adulthood, in the midlife years—and the knitting goes on in our mature years. That knitting goes on even in our final dying and in death itself. We step back now to observe that divine masterpiece with all its flaws. We come to know, appreciate and reverence our own story.

This is often no easy thing. But we can do it under the inspiration of the One who knit each of us. We re-member, re-work our story because often, we find that there is unfinished business back there influencing our present, and it needs to be attended to at this time. We re-member because each of us is as much our past as we are our present and our future. We know who we are by knowing our story.

Janice had a wonderful healing and comforting dream a while ago. We'll tell the story in her own words.

> My mother, Grace, was dead eight years at the time of this dream. She had died in a nursing home after being there ten months in a semicomatose state. I had felt badly about my mother being in a nursing home. At the time, and long after, all the events that led up to her being there lay heavy on my heart. And this, despite the fact that I had really grieved and worked through the stages of death and dying. I had also earlier been graced by messages of healing comfort from my own unconscious. Mary, a friend of mine, was able to take care of her mother who lived well beyond ninety. When Mary's mother was in need of greater care and presence, Mary took a leave of absence from her work and became her mother's support as well as caretaker. I regretted that I had not been able to do that. Often my heart would cry, "Oh, Mother, if only I had been a Mary." One Easter night I had this dream.

I was standing in the kitchen at the sink. I heard someone behind me and turned to see who it could be. It was my Mother. She was wearing a pink dress. She said, "What can I do for you, Janice?" I said, "Forgive me, Mother." My Mother answered, "You are forgiven, Janice."

The kitchen is symbolically the place of transformation. It was also my mother's room. She was a great cook, and I have many memories of her in a kitchen. The sink holds the water used in feeding and cleaning. Why my mother was wearing a pink dress is something I puzzle over. Pink is the traditional feminine color. It is also an Easter color. My mother wore a pink dress at the celebration of my 25th anniversary celebration as a Sister of Saint Joseph.

Someone pointed out to me that my mother was "behind me because she was and still is behind me all the way." My mother understood and appreciated my life's work. As I said, my mother was already dead eight years at the time of the dream. I thought I had worked through the stages of grieving very well. But our relationship with the dead is still in process and my unconscious in the dream was bringing me forward through yet another door in the relationship between my mother and myself. Placed in the context of Easter, the Easter apparitions, the suffering and death of Jesus, the forgiveness of Jesus for those who killed Him, and for the disciples who deserted Him, the dream was also putting my Mother's story into the context of the larger archetypal story of the life of Christ. My Mother's assurance of forgiveness, having been already given, may be pointing to my need to accept what has already been given, as well as to forgive myself.

The Greater Self knows what it is that we each need at any moment. In this dream, my mother is a Christ figure, assuring me of forgiveness. My greater Self is cleansing me once again of the ill effects of my neglect and failure. The Self is assuring me of pardon and transformation in and through Grace's suffering and death and now, of her new life. Those last years and months were for her, indeed, soulmaking years, and she, like Jesus, is in glory now.

The unconscious comes to us in our time of need to bring us to change and transformation. Our story is never over. The past is not simply the past. It is present and still in process. My mother came to me, gift of my unconscious, in my dream to give me her compassion, comfort and blessing and move me into my future. Was she the Christ? The Archetypal Self? Healing, forgiving, confirming?

The author, Mary Gordon, shared the story of her mother's later years with the whole world when she wrote about her mother in the magazine section of the *New York Times*. Mrs. Gordon had had a hard life but was able to pick herself up, become a career woman and provide a good family life for herself and Mary. In those active years, Mrs. Gordon had accomplished many, many things, not the least, that of raising her wonderfully gifted daughter. Yet, aging for Mrs. Gordon became a stumbling block. She ceased to care for herself or others.

Once, Mary tells us, Mrs. Gordon had neglected to remove her shoes for months and her feet became infected. Mary was pained and perplexed by her mother's attitude and behavior. She remembered her as a woman of vigor and activity. One day Mary pointed out to her mother that, indeed, she should not be like this. Could she not remember all the wonderful things she had once achieved despite the odds? Mary's mother simply answered, "That was then. This is now." Mrs. Gordon had come to identify herself totally with her present situation, with her ailing, frail body. She had no genuine felt sense for her whole Self: past, present, and future, but only her body. She identified herself with aging and decline. She was totally disconnected from the woman she had been, and in truth, still was. She appeared to be disconnected from the Self. She was totally alienated from her past, her own story. Any one of us who becomes alienated from our story seems disinhabited, in a sense, gone, an empty shell. We are devoid of sentiment. We are disassociated from our own successes, our own achievements, our own idealism, life goals, character, uniqueness. We seem to have given up the struggle of the integrity/despair polarity that leads to Wisdom.

Mary is a renowned storyteller, but she, Mrs. Gordon, has no story to tell. No story holds together and unifies the seasons of her life. This is the attitude of so much of the culture. Yet, when a sense of integrity for who you are and for all you have been intersects with a legitimate sense of despair that comes about because of the losses experienced: health, friends, spouses, careers, works, vitality, etc., the gift of Wisdom can come to birth. Without the integrity that comes from the Self alive in and

. through all we have experienced, we lose our soul. Disdain for life itself and an identification with despair itself is the worst scenario for someone who lives a lengthy life. In the Erickson's theory it is the interaction, the friction between our experiences of both integrity and despair that will bring Wisdom. They see Wisdom as the virtue of the last stage of life, the fruit of a lifetime.

We must accept the invitation now, "To take down the love letters from the shelves." Come to re-member ourselves. Put ourselves together once again by getting to know and see the making of our own Soul in and through our life experience. Come to see the Self still at work in our own creation now. When we were put together in our mother's womb by God, we were not complete. We continue to be knit in all the stages and seasons of our long life. We need bumper stickers that read: *God is not finished with me yet. Work in progress. Reconstruction Underway.*

The poet William Butler Yeats tells us:

> An aged man is but a paltry thing,
> A tattered coat upon a stick, unless
> Soul clap its hands and sing and louder sing. . . .
> ("Sailing to Byzantium" 1983:193)

And Soul is made in life, in poetry, in story. The whole world saw Soul in an impressionable little girl woman, Ann Frank, and again in the imprisoned young woman, Hettie Hillesum in the concentration camp. Soul and Self hold each of us together in the living. Soul and Self are the fruit of all life, but most especially, long life. We become the poets of our past lives. We become the poets of our now and of our tomorrow. Poet yourself to life, old man, old woman. Live these mature years, the womb of the Self.

The Spiritual Significance of Synchronicity

There are many times throughout our midlife years and the mature years that we need to be reminded that our Soul is leading us on the way; that, indeed, we are not alone. The psyche has many ways of directly assisting us in this re-member-ing that is called for at special moments in life.

Synchronicity is a term coined by Jung referring to a meaningful non-causal relationship between psychic and physical events. When there are two simultaneous meaningful occurrences that have no causal connection, we have a synchronistic event, a coincidence. Synchronicity suggests a continuum between the spiritual and physical levels of reality. Synchronistic events always have a powerful effect upon the Soul. Through them, with them, we have no doubt that God is near and that we are being led.

Often we find that in the midst of our struggles, our breakdowns, our efforts to reach out, reach in, or move beyond, an incident occurs to reassure us that we are beholden, we are not alone. Such an incident is recorded in Paula D'Arcy's book, *Gift of the Red Bird: A Spiritual Encounter*. In the frustration, pain and doubt, battling loneliness and depression during the initial withdrawal phase of a "vision quest," a brilliant red bird flew into Paula's life. After that brief surprise introduction, the red bird often hovered around her. Sometimes he sat at her feet contentedly and sang. As her solitary days progressed, the red bird remained with Paula and was a steadfast comfort. He often flew away, but always returned. These sudden reappearances were reassuring, and she grew to know that he was never far away. Initially, Paula had been drawn to embark on a wilderness experience, but she was not a solitary and had both attraction and repulsion for the solitude and loneliness that accompanied a wilderness experience. The red bird was exactly what Paula needed.

One day a tornado was approaching, and a man from the vision quest team came to evacuate Paula from her camping position to a place of safety. Her refuge was an empty bunkhouse, three-fourth's of a mile away from her site. As the team member left, he instructed her, "If the tornado approaches this spot, get into the bathtub and pull the mattress over your head."

After a long night of inner and outer turmoil, Paula awakened. The storm had passed. The danger was over. As Paula opened the door to start her hike back to her camping site, a flash of color at her feet startled her. "There on the doorstep waiting, was the red bird," Paula recalled. "Tears spilled from my eyes and I could barely breathe. How could he possibly know where to find me, or that this very doorstep was mine? The storm was one display of power. His waiting for me another. Such a moment is a gift" (119).

Whenever we are struggling with our story, our past, our present, our future, the creator is near. This is a moment of creative ferment, our ongoing creation is taking place here at this sacred moment. This is birthing time and these are the pains of the birthing labor. The psyche has a way of attracting nature and the physical universe. We, ourselves, are participating in nature and in the present moment, far beyond our consciousness and our own personal psychic reality.

Whenever we have a synchronistic event like the gift of the red bird, we stand in wonder and awe. We know we are not alone. We are beholden. Earlier in her book, Paula said, "When the brilliant red bird flew by, he took my breath away." Breath is spirit, breath is life and energy, breath is creation and re-creation. Breath is God. The red bird was about taking Paula's breath away. He was cleaning her and replenishing her very Soul. After a journey of forty, eighty, or ninety years, we, too, need to be cleansed and replenished. We, too, need to know that in the story we are living out, we are not alone. We live and breathe the divine life of a compassionate all-present God.

Peggy and Bill were "sweethearts" when they were fourteen (Peggy) and sixteen (Bill). But by the time Bill went into the service and fought in World War II, Peggy was engaged to another young man. Nevertheless her long relationship to Bill had her writing to this long-time friend, as well as to her fiancé, both fighting in the war. Bill was fighting in Belgium, and at this time he and three other men were housed in a small farmhouse. When orders came, and they were pulled out of Belgium, they had no time to return to the farmhouse for any of their belongings. When the war was over and Bill returned, Peggy broke off her engagement and married Bill. Speaking of Bill, Peggy said, "We had a deliriously happy marriage. I loved him more when he died that when I married him."

Bill died at sixty-eight after a two-year battle with cancer. Five years later, Peggy was diagnosed with cancer. She was terribly frightened and bewildered. She longed for her husband Bill. She missed the comfort, strength, companionship, and support he had always given her.

In the midst of this acute loneliness and faced with all the decisions that she needed to make with regard to her cancer, Peggy felt abandoned. She was in a "dark night of the soul." She was comfortless, fatigued, weary, fearful, and desolate. She longed for Bill. At the moment when her longing was most intense, a letter came from Pierre Godeau of Vauxaur-Sure, Belgium. Something like fifty years after Bill had left Belgium, Peggy gets a letter asking her if she would be interested in receiving the letters she had sent Bill during the war. Whenever Peggy talked about this miraculous moment, it gave her "chills." "It was like someone had put courage in an envelope and mailed it to me. I can't tell you. The way I interpreted it was that he was thinking of me, saying 'Get a grip, Peg. I'm right here.' So I had the operation, and I have chemotherapy every week. I'm hanging in."

Pierre Godeau had been put in charge of a memorial in Bastogne in Belgium and was searching for memorabilia. A woman in the farmhouse that had billeted Bill offered him some memorabilia from the Battle of the Bulge. With it was a leather bag containing the perfectly preserved letters that had been sent to Private William Guditus. Most of the letters were the letters Peggy had written to her friend Bill. Pierre took the leather case and searched for the whereabouts of Bill. Peggy received Pierre's letter at precisely the right time. She needed to re-member.

Ira Progoff has an exercise in his journal called "Roads Taken or Not Taken." This exercise has us see how different our lives would be if we did not take the path we took. Peggy had a wonderful life with Bill. Her numerous children, grandchildren, and great-grandchildren are the fruit of that wonderful union. But it could have been otherwise.

Looking back at the early romance of these childhood sweethearts, we realize that for Peggy and Bill it was an early experience of being "soul mates." Even though at the time of the war Peggy was engaged to another soldier, she kept up her relationship with Bill and wrote to him faithfully. It was as if her ego had chosen another man to marry, but her soul would not let go of her early friendship. Peggy's greater Self maintained her close affective feelings for her childhood sweetheart. Their exchange of letters, which were truly "love letters," prepared Peggy for breaking off her engagement and marrying her first, and really, *only* soul mate.

This is what Peggy needed to remember. She needed to be put in contact with her greater Self. The Self had engineered Peggy's marriage. It was in that marital relationship that Peggy matured as a woman. There Peggy developed in relationship, in love, in giftedness, in creativity. The greater Self had brought Peggy through the loss of Bill, and she would carry Peggy through her cancer and chemotherapy. All was and is Soul making.

Bill's letters gave Peggy the sure awareness that, indeed, Bill was with her, rooting for her. The letters were a great symbol of God's providential care for her. Peggy's letters to Bill were the letters of her Soul. Peggy's Self chose to be faithful to her friendship and write to Bill all during the war. Peggy's ego chose someone else to marry; but Peggy's Soul chose Bill and would not let him go. This synchronistic event of the arrival of the letters brought home to Peggy the loving presence of Bill, the abiding presence of her Self. Both were very much alive and with her at this moment of crisis. Peggy knew, "I am not alone. No one is alone." "All is well, all manner of things will be well." We need to re-member. We need to "take down the love letters from the shelf."

SIX

Staying Generative

The Virtue of Care—Contemplative Living

In chapter two there is a poem called "The Rose." The poem is about the human life story in all its stages from infancy through death and beyond. Three of the lines that refer especially to the second half of life are these:

> Stay, stay why do you let the bees eat?
> Almost full circle; heart all given
> Letting go again, one petal at a time.

As I wrote those words, I was outdoors and a great buzzing bee darted at my foot. I did not let the bee eat! The coincidence, the synchronicity of that tiny event underlines how concretely this is where I am in my life, and how the giving, working, caring that is going on is not without struggle and resistance on my part. The letting go, being eaten up of now is different. There is generativity in early adulthood, there is procreation and creations of all kinds. The responsible adult has learned to give. All the ego striving of the first part of adulthood taught us to give ourselves in so many ways, to let ourselves be eaten up. Parents are surely eaten up by the needs of their children. We give ourselves to our work. So often, doing it well consumes us. However, generativity continues long past the childbearing, child-rearing years, and long past the years of building our empires of home and work.

Continuing *care* for what one has generated and the generation and regeneration of oneself through continuing productivity and creativity are never finished for the growing adult. We tend to think of generativity in the narrow sense as what happens during the child-bearing, child-rearing years. Generating, creating something is, of course, just as essential to those who do not have children during those years. Yet, just like all the ego strengths of the previous stages, *care* needs to be constantly reworked again and again throughout life. We do this by struggling many times with the conflict in ourselves between generativity and stagnation. A social responsibility is always implicit in the individuation process of any truly growing person, if that person is to live a fully realized life; if a person is to have passion for life.

This becomes harder now because we have spent so many years working and giving, learning and giving. People have been eaten up by children and bosses and schedules and demands, demands, demands. There is a great temptation to say, "enough already, I deserve to be taken care of now." Of course there is a certain truth to this, the caretaker in us does need to give way to other aspects, other long-neglected parts of ourselves. However, there is a dangerous and deadening attitude that has been prevalent in our society that contributes to the age mystique, and negative image of old age. Richard Bolles talks about it in *The Three Boxes of Life*. He tells us that in our culture today there is an orgy of *learning* in the first part of life, an orgy of *work* in the second part of life, followed by an orgy of *leisure* in the last. His thesis is that we need a degree of all three in each stage of life. In later adulthood, we need learning, work, and leisure. Certainly, there is a difference in the amount of time and of myself given to work than in early adulthood, and a difference in the amount of time given to learning than in childhood. Yet this is not simply and exclusively a time for an orgy of leisure.

The Eriksons suggest that the virtue of Care is acquired in adulthood by bearing the tension between generativity and stagnation. There needs to be both generativity and stagnation. One-sided generativity with no stagnation, that is, with no stillness, no leisure, no liminality, no contemplation is not true generativity.

The midlife crisis often overtakes a person with feelings of deadness, monotony, boredom, apathy, lethargy. People feel as if they are stagnating. Many people say that they feel becalmed, dead. It is possible to die at forty or fifty, and not get buried until ninety-five. It is possible to get stuck in these feelings, and never make the midlife transition. It is even possible for someone who made a good transition to experience these feelings again at other times during the second half of life. Retirement, especially after its initial honeymoon stage is over, can be a catalyst for being overwhelmed by stagnation.

From a Jungian perspective, when such feelings come over a person, energy is being drained away from a person's conscious concerns and given over to the unconscious so that new things can be readied to move into consciousness. New aspects of the personality are being empowered to grow. This can happen several times during the second half of life. Yet there is always a danger. Any crisis is both peril and potential. One can always choose to surrender totally to stagnation. The movement toward individuation is blocked.

John had had it with being the great provider. He retired not only from his job but from everything. Widowed, he wanted no entanglements. He would have none of this "grandfather business" either. The idea of being "grandfather" is repugnant to many. The title: "grandfather," "grandmother" has thrown many people into crisis. It becomes the herald of the fact of their aging. John said over and over again that he just wanted to be *"left alone."* He just wanted to *"veg out."* He moved to the sunbelt, "far from all of them." He could not be bothered cooking for himself or dressing to go out. Most days, he did not bother dressing at all. The television was his life and an occasional trip to the races, until even that became too much trouble. Year after year his health and appearance deteriorated. He was having "his time" but he was prematurely dead, stagnating, stuck. Eventually, John took his own life.

Unfortunately, John is not an isolated case. The suicide rate for men in their seventies is high. Even though the suicide rate for women is lower, it is still alarmingly high. Drug and alcohol abuse can be a different form of the same thing, a slower form of suicide, an oblivion—emotional and practical. It becomes a drowning, a narrowing of consciousness rather than an expansion of consciousness. In an exchange of letters between Carl Jung and Bill Wilson, the cofounder of Alcoholics Anonymous, Jung told Wilson that he believed that the alcoholic was caught in a search for *spirit* in the wrong place. He pointed out that the Latin word for alcohol is "spiritus," that is, "spirit." He congratulated Wilson on the spiritual insight in the twelve steps. The admission of powerlessness, and turning oneself over to a Higher Power, certainly reflects the surrender of the ego to the lead of the greater Self, the Image of God, the God within as well as the God outside.

Our "three boxes of life" society fails to give the message that growth and generativity, learning and working are always a part of life. Retirement is another crisis time in the sense of peril or potential. John had been the great provider. He had given himself completely to his work, "doing it all for the wife and kids." Now at retirement, he has an experience from the other side of his personality, from his shadow side, his long neglected side. The exact opposite of the hard worker and caregiver comes up into his consciousness with great force because it had so long been denied. He feels the strong desire to "veg out," to just take it easy, to live for himself, not for others. In John's case and unfortunately in the case of all too many retirees, he simply allowed this new part of himself, this new experience of his other side to eat him up, to collapse his ego. The hard worker, provident, husband/father becomes totally disengaged from everyone and everything. John's sense of this being the time to take it easy, and to start living more for himself certainly was the right one for him, after all it came from deep within himself. It was a shadow experience engineered by the Self. However, this shadow experience, like any shadow experience, needed to be integrated not swallowed whole. He literally just let himself go. He was consumed by the shadow. How could he have integrated his genuine need for a life of more leisure, more privacy, and time to do what he wanted and needed to do? The unconscious needs the conscious, the planning and will of our ego to make real its suggestions.

Bill Blass, whom we wrote about earlier, and most other women and men, like John, begin to get all kinds of inner messages from their psyches and bodies to begin to slow down and just be; to think more about their own needs at this time of life. Bill Blass started leaving New York City for the country each weekend. Thousands of others, less affluent, have found their own ways—gardening, fishing, reading, meditating, praying, listening to music, photography, just looking and listening—without letting go of all the other needs for relationships, productivity, and creativity. Nor without letting go of developing new and different dimensions of themselves, skills, values, goals, dreams—generativity in its broadest sense. The unconscious needs the discernment of the ego about *how much* leisure how much stagnation or how much of anything is *too much.*

We can take the seemingly negative word, *stagnation,* and see that it points to a much deeper reality—to contemplation. Living the second half of life well is living more contemplatively. It is living with more inwardness and interiority. We need to be more in touch with the deep-down things, with the Mystery at the core of everything, with the Mystery at the core of our being. There needs to be spaces in our active lives for the eternal to become manifest. There need to be times to recognize the epiphanies. Workaholism is the opposite of true generativity; so is materialism. Remaining active as we age for the sake of activity, spinning our wheels, risk taking, merely for an adrenaline rush, is not passion for life, is not generativity. Life is a great mystery. We need to make time to touch into that mystery. Age will give us this time. Real generativity will flow from the Greater Self that we are in the process of becoming. It will be an *expression* of our uniqueness, a revelation of the unique Image of God that each of us is. It will flow out of stillness. It will require taking long, loving looks at what is. It will require times of reflection, meditation, contemplation.

This whole book has been a contemplation of life in its aspect as eternal and mysterious Otherness. As we age, there needs to be more and more times of contemplation. As the eternal breaks through our bodies and souls, we will find ourselves communing with life on a whole different level. We will find that there is an ongoing dialogue and communication with the Mystery beyond and behind, above and below, it all. Ultimately, we will be communing with the God of it all. "Pray always," says the scripture. Prayer is the lifting of the whole person—body, mind, heart, soul, and spirit to God. This God is the God beyond all names—all words—who transcends everything: yet is immanent in everything. True prayer will go on in our religious rituals and beyond them. As the eternal breaks through our bodies and souls, even our playing and working can become a kind of praying as we grow in wholeness and become more centered. Our generativity will grow from this place of stillness. Then it will be true care. It will be true love.

Passion for Life is passion for the fullness of Life. It is passion for living fully. "The glory of God is the human person fully alive," says second-century St. Ireneus. It is passion, too, for the eternal in humanity.

"Live on as though you had centuries," says Jung. Live on as though you had eternal life, says the ancient Wisdom of the religions of the world. It will be in our times of contemplation and in our contemplative living that this can become real to each of us. Life will forge our Wisdom Prayers:

In the stillness of my expectant heart, let Wisdom arise, O God.
In the midst of turmoil, conflict and suffering, let Wisdom arise, O God.
In joy and ectasy, let Wisdom arise, O God.
In the fullness of life and in each diminishment, let Wisdom arise, O God.
As this life draws to an end and new life approaches, let Wisdom arise, O God.
Spirit of Wisdom, when I am in the midst of experiencing my own sin and evil
give me the Wisdom to know my own goodness.
When I am inflated and identify with my own goodness,
blinded to my own evil and sin,
give me the Wisdom to know the truth.
Great Wisdom, abiding in me, create me anew,
bring me to my own fullness and the fullness of time.
Wisdom, let me be the source of bringing others
and this world of ours to the fullness of time. Amen.

"I have come so that you may have life and have it to the full," says Jesus (John 10:10).

Generativity in creative tension with all the positive benefits of its opposite, *just being* or contemplation in its broadest sense is a spirituality of genuine love. This is true love of self and neighbor. It is the Charity or *agape* of the Christian; the Compassion of Buddhism; the *Hesed* of Judaism. It is the core of all religious living. Generativity, for the adult in life's second half is concerned for the next generations. It is passing on the consciousness that one continues to increase. True consciousness always includes behavior. One's consciousness is never truly increased until one begins to act out of the new consciousness. Generativity is enriching the future while I am here. Generativity happens in all kinds of ways.

Elderhostel is an educational program for elders who take over empty college and university dorms and classrooms and faculty on break. Lois Brunner Bastian in *Modern Maturity* magazine quotes two forty-something Ph.D. professors who look forward to learning from the elder students whom they teach. "Hostelers ask questions that push teachers to the edge; they challenge assumptions faculty members take for granted. Teaching elder hostel is a gift I give myself," said Dr. Jack Harris. His colleague, Dr. Rocco Capraro looks forward to the same kind of challenge. He is sparked by hostelers' love of learning. "As a group, they are sure of who they are and they're secure, having successfully navigated life's obstacles. So they speak out more freely because they're not awed by the teacher or fearful about disagreeing with him or her." Both teachers obviously find this different from undergraduates who are still unsure of themselves and inexperienced in living life. Of course, both professors strongly dispute the stereotype of mature students not being able to consider new ideas. There is real reciprocity here. These older adults are willing to learn from the younger professors. Yet, it is the younger professors who say here that they give themselves the gift of teaching in Elderhostel Programs because they get so much from the elders whom they teach. They get so much encouragement and support in their love for their own subject, so much insight and challenge, so much affirmation in the very act of teaching. This is generativity on the side of teachers and of students.

Elderhostel and some other learning situations designed specifically for adult learners is an important new development. Most universities open their courses for audit by older learners at no fee or a very reduced fee. Many offer credit courses at reduced fees. This is an important trend not only for the elders but for the young students and the teachers. These are our tribal elders. Our Tribal Elders are those who have become more conscious and more aware by having examined and contemplated their experiences and having learned from them. In tribal cultures, the elders are the guardians of the laws and the rites of passage and the mysteries. They are the tellers of tales, passing on the traditions, the sacred aspects of the culture that give meaning to life. Having passed on their learning through their own experience of life, our elders today can mediate their own inner priorities to the young and give a new dignity to learning. They have a special ability to make nonmaterial reality come alive for the young.

Some businesses are wisely calling some of their retirees back to work as consultants, so that newer, younger personnel can benefit from their experience and creativity. Of course, such companies are exceptional, since many more companies are committed to downsizing through forced retirement. In general, there are almost no institutional vehicles in our society for taking advantage of the wisdom of our elders. Perhaps, the most noteworthy exception to this has been the Supreme Court of the United States. However, there are all kinds of informal vehicles, and the sheer numbers of generative aging in the society is having its leavening effect.

In the "three boxes of life," learning is a crucial form of ongoing generativity. Curiosity is a form of the vital life force, the vitality that has moved humanity forward. It is also a vital force that always keeps one growing and changing. Curiosity is the élan of spirit moving the infant to crawl out and the adult to learn something new. The curious adult in life's second half is a listener and a learner. He or she is willing to let go of competition for the spotlight in order to hear what a peer is saying.

He or she is willing to give up competition with the young to "sit at their feet" and learn anything in which they have expertise. He or she is curious about what makes the next generation tick and will be open to the new mores, language, values, music, and art that humanity is evolving in the new generations. People who are aging well are letting go of personal competition in general, since, while competition may have its place in the ego building of the first half of life, it has very little if any place in the becoming of the Self. Soulmaking is uniqueness making. Souls cannot be measured over against anything. This is the time when we are withdrawing our projections from both our heroes and demons and discovering them in ourselves. If we are growing, we have begun to notice in ourselves more of those traits, both the good ones and the bad ones, that we overlooked in ourselves, but never missed in other people. This both frees us to stop measuring ourselves over and against others and makes it possible to *learn* from all kinds of other people.

It is the rigid, stuck older adult who sees only the flaws in the next generation. Stuck people are like a broken record who repeat again and again: "They are all immoral, promiscuous drug addicts. Their language and music are barbaric. One never saw the likes in my day." This kind of an attitude effectively cuts off any discriminating about what is really going on in the next generation. It can make a person blind and deaf to the world of one's present. The most tragic suicide of all is this kind of killing of the spark of curiosity, and of respect for the new, just because it is new.

Learning from both the past and the present can expand the personality. The desire to know, the need to understand is part of the thrust toward expanding our consciousness, expanding human consciousness. It can always be a source of new dynamism.

Typology: A Key to New Growth and Creativity

Besides all there is still to learn in the areas and fields that have always interested us, there are for each person whole areas of human knowledge and behaviors that were virtually untouched in the first half of life because of our personality type. There is so much undiscovered self. For so many people, whom we have met in our Mid-Life Directions and Long Life Directions Workshops, Jung's theory of typology sheds light on why they have suddenly become interested in exploring things and doing things that in their youth they had shunned and even laughed at.

"Why have I become interested in birds? When I think about it, I feel like a fool. When I was younger, I thought bird watching was inane. Now I've gone and bought binoculars, so I can get a better look at them, and a book to help me recognize them," an embarrassed, burley, retired entrepreneur said.

A fiftyish woman who had never before in her life been involved in sports told us that she had recently become interested in tennis and "even more unbelievably in pro football." She had gone to a few games and was enjoying watching it on television, even though she still did not understand all the rules and knew very little about any of the teams. "I can't believe myself," she said, "I despised jocks and looked down on anyone who was a fan! My husband is even more amazed at me."

A man in very avant-garde outfit said that he always drove a flashy car, usually a red Jaguar, but that he had recently bought a much more "sensible model." He went on to tell us with an amazed disbelief that he found himself doing all kinds of practical, down-to-earth, sensible things, "even, dressing a lot less flamboyantly!" Looking at his clothes, we wondered what more flamboyant would be like. "Until I heard about this type thing," he said, I was really afraid, I was becoming a boring, old fuddy-duddy. My family and friends, however, seem relieved. My kids say I'm less of a space cadet."

Someone else who was never *mechanical and* always *hired people to fix whatever needed to be fixed said that he had recently fixed a door that had never closed securely, then he started building a deck, and refinishing an old antique ice box. "I'm determined to finish both these jobs and I feel high about it all. It's as if I'd climbed Mount Everest," he said.*

Another woman had started gardening. "No one who knows me can believe it. When I got excited about my red impatience they laughed at me. My sister said, 'You never knew an impatience from a petunia.'"

Someone else said, "I've started studying the Civil War but I was never interested in either history or facts. I wouldn't be caught dead watching a game show or playing Trivial Pursuit."

In Jung's theory of psychological types all of these people above were **Intuitive types,** either *Extraverted* Intuitives (the "Jaguar" man) or Introverted Intuitives (the "football" woman) who have begun to be caught into their undeveloped sensing side. We all perceive, take in reality through our senses and through our intuition. We generally rely on one at the expense of the other. In the first half of life, we tend to develop one more than the other. Then in life's second half, for wholeness and individuation, we need to develop the opposite. Since this need is inbuilt, we can begin to feel attracted to things we hardly knew or cared existed when we were younger. At one extreme, we can experience life primarily through our bodies, our senses. What is real, what we notice and are attracted to is what we can see, or hear, or taste, or smell. Anything else seems fanciful, impractical, irrelevant to the real business of living life.

On the other extreme, is our intuitive function. Jung defines intuition as perception through the unconscious. Intuitives perceive more through their intuition than through their senses. What they are conscious of is much more what comes to them intuitively than what their senses have to tell them. The unconscious is the womb of potentials and new possibilities. Its language is images, symbols, metaphor. It is the seat of imagination. Intuitives are always perceiving possibilities, probabilities, and potentials through the unconscious, often even noticing what is unconscious but potential in other people. What's possible has a certain palpable presence for them. They love images, metaphors, symbols, myths, and imagination. Intuitives may miss what is right under their noses but see connections and what is on the way. They are much more future-oriented than present-oriented. People say, *"The intuitive cannot see the trees for the forest."*

Since Intuitives are conscious of potentials and possibilities, they can easily imagine outcomes. Introverted Intuitives always see the other side of everything. They can be aware of subtle nuances and cues long before others notice them. They pick up vibes, have hunches, always have their antenna out. Extraverted Intuitives see what is coming next, want to be into "what's hot," the new trends, what is right around the corner. They have a passion for new ideas, they are always aware of what *might be* rather than what *is.* They are the entrepreneurs always starting something new. They are caught into successive projects. Their enthusiasm for their current projects knows no bounds of energy or time, and can be very infectious, yet it may soon peter out when something new attracts them. Introverted and Extraverted Intuitives tend to be bored by facts and hate repetition. When they do notice facts and details, they often spin them into new theories or projects. Since they do not have much sense of the present, they miss many details in their surroundings. Since they do not have a good sense of time, they tend to take on too many things at once. Making a hamburger could lead to preparing tomorrow's dinner and cleaning the refrigerator, all with only a half hour at their disposal. They are more conscious of the future than the present. They tend to have little awareness of their bodies, often do not notice when they are sick or tired, and they may not have much interest in sports. Patience, especially the kind of patience that is required to build or fix things, is not their strong suite. They would rarely be called conservative and are apt to be impractical. In clothes, cars, and indeed most areas of life, they do not often choose on the basis of the practical, the conservative, or the thing that is the most sensible.

Knowing these things about Intuitives makes it easier to understand why the people, whose stories we used as illustrations above, were rather surprised at their new experiences of themselves. Each of them was operating out of their long-neglected, less-developed, sensing side. All through the second half of life, the unconscious, dormant, neglected, undeveloped side of our personalities keeps emerging from consciousness; we can heed, welcome, nurture, include, integrate its invitations or ignore them and continue to let them fall back into oblivion. We need to work at accepting those things that were dormant within us and once unacceptable to us. The example of the man who was *afraid* that he was becoming an "old fuddy-duddy" because he was beginning to dress more conservatively, as well as use his more practical, sensible, stable, less future-oriented sensing side, shows what resistance can interfere with this integration of our shadow functions.

Often in the first half of life when we are developing our own gifts we tend to look down on and to dislike those who have the opposite gifts. Intuitives who are always into new and futuristic thinking and projects while they tend to miss many facts, call Sensing people boring, obsessive, drab, predictable, or drones. Sensing peoples who are fact-oriented and practical see Intuitives as flaky, "air heads," unreal, flighty, impatient, impractical.

Therefore I can tend to be frightened when this despised opposite appears in myself. I can suppress the slightest hints of the emergence of this "flighty side" of my formerly predictable self, or run away from the emerging new predictability of my ever-innovative self. However, if I risk going with this seduction from the other side of my personality when it draws me again and again throughout the second half of life, I will mellow, and become more and more integrated. I will stay dynamic, alive, curious, passionate about life. I will become more whole. I will not be so one-sided, so judgmental. Most of all, I will have a whole new world to explore. The side of the world that was closed to me in the first half of my life will begin to open up for me. That world can be a source of new dynamism and tremendous new energy. I will never make this opposite personality style completely my own, it will even continue to cause me trouble because I will never be as skilled in it as I am in my native personality style. In spite of this it can give me moments of ecstasy as I go where I never went before.

If I was into Sensing in the first part of my life because that was my gift, I was into facts, practicality, the concrete here and now. I may have become an accountant, engineer, a bookkeeper, a transportation manager, librarian, sportcaster, lab technician because this suited my Sensing, factual bent. Now, in the second half of life a whole new world awaits my exploration.

In Jung's personality theory, totally surrendering one side of myself for the other is not healthy development. No matter how burned out I am as a bookkeeper, I should not totally jump to the other side and become a full-time fashion designer in an avant-garde house because I just loved my first adult education course in fashion design! Perhaps though, I should begin to experiment with a less practical and sensible way of dressing. Total abandonment of my own gifts is destructive to the ego. It is collapse of the ego. We do not change by exchanging our conscious for our unconscious selves. We do not exchange Sensing for Intuition or visa versa. Yet, we do allow our intuitive self to have some place in our lives.

Our basic personality type always remains the same. We do not switch from one type to the other. However, in the process of individuating, growing in wholeness, becoming more and more our Self, we integrate the opposites of our highly developed attitude and functions. Integrating the opposites is transformative, like the leaven in the dough. It is a case of making new friends but keeping the old.

We move beyond stagnation when we try frequently to risk using those parts of ourselves with which we have no expertise. We will perhaps have to give ourselves the freedom to feel or look foolish. We will need to let ourselves make the mistakes of a learner. There is indeed real pain and discomfort involved in growth. Our ego wants to continue limiting our consciousness in the interest of focus and adaptation, and keeping our "in control" persona intact. Here, we need the Child archetype to come alive in us to help the adult we are to try something new. The child is always messing up as it crawls out over and over again to explore something new. The child unabashedly picks itself up again and again as it's learning to walk and to ride a bike. Otherwise, it is never free to move on and move out.

In every Sensing person, the world of intuition is always a potential. Now in the second half of life, the world of the imaginative, the symbolic, the world of possibilities and potentials, the world of the general rather than the particular, open up before them. When it does, and they respond and go with it, art, in all its facets, music in all its magnificence, poetry, and even fantasy and imagination, may become more important to the Sensing persons. They may become more interested in things like science fiction and in futuristic space fantasies. They may begin to let themselves go more in imagery, symbolism, idle speculation, and day dreams. They may even "buy Jaguars" or other sports cars, though probably not red ones. An Introverted Sensing friend in his fifties *leased a dark blue* Jaguar after a lifetime of owning what he called "sensible cars." They may become more interested in spiritual disciplines and things philosophical. They may begin to dress a bit less sensibly and more fashionably. They may risk doing something on a whim more often.

One Introverted Sensing man drove across country to a midlife workshop that we were giving. He told us that for the first time he had not carefully planned the trip down to the last detail as he had always done before. He had not made any motel reservations. He traveled "as the spirit moved him and stayed wherever he landed each night." He was so proud of what he called his new freedom.

Another Introverted Sensing woman told us that she had shared a vacation cottage with other members of her family. Every summer when it came time to open the cottage, she would go a day or more early and scrub everything until it was "shipshape." Then she would spend her two weeks annoyed at the carelessness of her sister and all the other family members "who were always messing things up." Finally, one year when she was in her fifties, her husband persuaded her to go a day *after* everyone else and to take things as she found them. She told us that since then she has enjoyed her vacations there so much more. She is acquiring some of the casualness and flexibility that characterizes her shadow type, which is Extraverted Intuitive.

An Extraverted Sensing man lost his job of thirty years in his fifties because of a downsizing in his company. He was devastated. By chance, he saw a brochure for a dream workshop, something he would always have ignored and thought to be "kooky" before this moment. He and his wife went to the workshop and were fascinated by it. This prodded him to start paying attention to his dreams and the spontaneous images that came to him. He began reading in a whole new area. This led him to the video series, *The Power of Myth* with anthropologist Joseph Campbell. He was profoundly moved by these Bill Moyers interviews with Campbell. This became a year's spiritual quest during which he started imagining a different future for himself. He laughed at himself when he thought about how any long-range planning of the future had always terrified him in the past. He took Campbell's advice to "follow your bliss" and started his own business with new enthusiasm and great optimism. Wisely however, the business was in the kind of information gathering field that was familiar to him. Yet the risk involved in being an entrepreneur was a real stretching for him.

Interest in dreams, images, myths; futuring, following one's bliss, becoming an entrepreneur—all this is the realm of the Intuitive. I have an Intuitive friend who has a banner that says, "You are what you dream yourself to be." I have a Sensing friend who has a plaque on her desk that reads, "Facts not fluff." True to his type, this entrepreneur started a business that was a very fact-oriented one. However, he had more respect now for "people who read between the lines, live in their heads, and focus on the unseen." He had begun ever so hesitantly, to read between a few lines, himself.

We have only focused on this small part of Jung's theory of psychological types to give an example of the wholeness and new learning that can come from opening one's conscious ego to one's less conscious or unconscious dormant shadow typology. In Jung's view, this is an important part of the process of Individuation, the becoming of our own true Self. We see it also as a major part of generativity. A person who does nothing to integrate the opposite functions of his or her personality type is stagnating. This is a dangerous collapse of the important generativity/stagnation polarity that the Eriksons have explored, and a block in the individuation process that Jung names as a goal for the second half of life. This failure to integrate inferior functions keeps one from becoming more whole.

When the Sensing person does not begin to integrate the opposite, what was beautiful at thirty-five may become ugly by seventy-five. One woman, always responsible, precise, into details, and neatness found that in her seventies she could not get to sleep if all the shades in her house were not at exactly the same height and everything was not in its exact place. An Extraverted Sensing man, always fun loving, and a sports lover; the life of the party, with his tales of his exploits on the college football team began to seem very adolescent when this was still his major topic of conversation in his late sixties. The Intuitive who could not ever stay in one place found herself at fifty with a desperate ache to belong somewhere.

There is a great deal more to Jung's type theory. Beside the perceiving functions of Sensing and Intuition that we have just briefly discussed, Jung proposed that we use two other functions to make our decisions. We use Thinking and Feeling to react to our perceptions, to make our judgments. Again, we are more gifted for one over the other and we tend to develop our preferred judging function in the first half of life. This leaves the opposite in a more unconscious dormant, undeveloped state and makes it the source of potential growth in the second half of life.

In the story we told earlier about Ann Brennan senior learning to say, "I love you," for example, Thinking was her preferred and more conscious way of being. It was her Feeling function with which she was less comfortable. It was this less developed side that began to be more operative once she made her initial breakthroughs, one of which was calling her adult children to tell them for the first time that she loved them. Feeling is more personal and subjective. Thinking is more impersonal and objective. Like Ann, an English hospital administrator, another Thinker discovered more of her shadow, dormant feeling function later in life. She told us that before she retired she prided herself in running an efficient medical center. "One of my pet peeves," she said, "was long tea breaks. They always ran with half full cups when they saw me coming. Now that I've retired, I've been amazed at what wonderful things can happen over a cup of tea."

On the other hand, Feelers begin to need to assert themselves. They need more space from people, need to let those around them have their own conflicts without interfering and explaining them to one another. They need to be liberated from their many *shoulds*.

Joe Sanders was an Extraverted Feeler, and principal of the same school for more than sixteen years. Both parents and kids loved Mr. Sanders. He knew all the children in family after family, and had begun to be invited to their weddings. Well into midlife, Joe Sanders, never before much of a drinker, started having drinking bouts on some weekends. Many Friday nights, he would go off by himself to a bar, far from his school district, and far from his home, and drink heavily. Eventually, he started discovering on Saturday mornings that he had brought home things that he had obviously stolen. One Saturday, he found a bench in his yard that he realized he had brought home from somewhere. He made up his mind to go for help. In time, it came out that this dangerous and very uncharacteristic behavior of the lovable, "good guy," Joe Sanders was a kind of unconscious rebellion. This "drunken thief" was indeed Joe's shadow. It seems he realized that he was sick and tired of always living up to all "their and *his own* shoulds and oughts." This was a very destructive way of coming in touch with his long denied Thinker side. The Thinker would rarely if ever make any decision, as the Feeler would, to keep people happy and avoid conflict.

As we move through the second half of life, we need to suffer through bringing our inferior functions, the opposite of our favored, highly developed functions, to consciousness and acting out of them more frequently. If intuition is our strength, we need to experience life consciously through our senses. If relying on our senses keeps us unaware of potentials for changing things, we need our intuition to see the possibilities inherent in our situation. If our decisions are usually based on feeling, what we or others like and dislike, we need to be more objective, impersonal, and logical. If our decisions are usually based on logic and principle, we need to begin to see extenuating circumstances, and our own and other's values.

In his wonderful groundbreaking book, *Psychological Types,* Jung, besides naming our four typical psychological functions—Sensing, Intuition, Thinking, and Feeling—coined the now very common words, Introverted and Extraverted. Jung saw that people's psychic energy seemed to flow both inward toward the psyche (Introverted), and outward to the environment (Extraverted). While we all have the potential both to introvert and extrovert, we tend to be more gifted for one over the other. We often hear about very young children that he or she is very outgoing (Extraverted), or that he or she takes everything in (Introverted). If our conscious ego is more Extraverted in life's first half, we tend to be drawn by our more introverted side throughout the second half of life. On the other hand, those who were more introverted will tend to start to be more and more comfortable with their Extraverted side now. Again, this does not mean that we switch from one to the other, but that we integrate the other. Healthy development means that we do not allow ourselves to lose our gift.

If I am more Extraverted, I will continue to need a great deal of interaction and involvement with people, places, and things, even while I also allow more solitary times for things like retrospection, introspection, thinking, dreaming, ruminating, speculating, contemplating, just getting comfortable with myself. Too much of this unfamiliar inner territory will exhaust me, however. So I need to keep a balance. I need to be aware that I will be getting messages from my unconscious Introverted side— new feelings, desires, urges to spend more time alone. I need to heed these messages, and not run from them even while not collapsing my extroversion and becoming a recluse. There are many old people around who have made all the mistakes that are possible in going too far, or not far enough with this typological mellowing. As with the more Extroverted, so also with the more Introverted. They will be drawn to, and attracted to more interaction and involvement than they were comfortable with in the first half of their lives. Perhaps, they will begin to need a greater breath of relationships, more communication, will begin getting more active and interested in many more external things, seeking new experiences outside of themselves. They too need to use discernment, learn from the extroverts but not try to go too far toward becoming one. They too will be exhausted by too much of their opposite attitude.

Integration however is a process of trial *and* error. If it were easy everyone of a certain age would be beautifully whole. Yet, the process of integrating our, until now, more unconscious opposite attitude of Introversion or Extraversion, challenging as it is, becomes a movement toward life and growth. As I mellow in these ways, I am becoming more my Self. The alternative is one-sidedness and stagnation. In becoming more whole I have so much more to give back to the world in far more graceful ways. This knowledge of Jung's theory of typology becomes a kind of road map for ways in which I can and will grow as I move through the second half of life. Yet, while the invitation, the urge, and the impetus from the other side of my personality is built in, its integration is not automatic.

The emergence of the shadow type in me is archetypal. However, I need to go with the flow. Much of my resistance to this kind of growth will come from my own uncomfortableness, even downright dislike of this weaker side of me. I have perhaps, always disliked, even had contempt for those people who were gifted with the opposite attitude and functions from mine. For example, Extraverted people call those who are more Introverted bad names like: deadhead, slow, boring, dull, intense, secretive, wimp, so deep, you drown. The Extraverted people get called noisy, pushy, nosy, shallow, loud mouth, busybody, flake, or bossy. Now

I'm being called to embrace the "pushy flake" or the "mousy, secretive one" in myself. Therefore, I need the courage to get beyond my prejudice against what is really my own weaker side.

There is something in me that impels toward the development of the total personality. Life in me has a purposeful goal, my wholeness, my true Self. My ego, however, wants to continue limiting my consciousness, as it did in the first half of life to help me adapt to my environment, and to keep me focused. To embrace the opposites in people around me, or in myself will disturb my comfort level. So now my ego must suffer, as my consciousness expands. The pull toward stagnation, toward getting stuck is great. The becoming of the Self, the Image of God that I am and can be, will only come at a cost.

The Gift You Have Received, Give as a Gift

This time of adult life has so much to teach us and in the process we become vessels, consciously or unconsciously, to hold and pass on what we have learned of the world and life to the *world around* us. The combined learning and teaching of each generation is constantly gestating the culture that is passed on to the next. This is a miracle of human evolution that we hardly notice until the years of life's second half. Then, if we are alive at all, it looms very large. We have the big picture now. If we have begun in midlife to operate out of the other side of our typology, this broadens our perceptions even further, and our vistas are so much larger. Our scope is larger now. Our instrument is fine-tuned. Our explorations have become soul-sized. Jung has said that if the first half of life is for nature, the second half of life is for the culture.

A man who was and remained a true learner, worker, and master of creative leisure and contemplation and who was passionate about passing on what he had learned was Jacques Cousteau. Cousteau, the oceanographer, had studied the underwater world, he had always used television to share what he had learned but in the process he had always passed on his own passion for this mysterious world beneath the seas. He was both growing and generative.

I remember David Whyte, a poet and lecturer, saying that Cousteau was his hero. All through his childhood, he had watched television broadcasts about Cousteau's adventures at the bottom of the sea. He determined that he too would become an oceanographer. However, when he went to make application for his oceanography major, he found that the schools that taught it were so full that he could not get in anywhere. He decided that half the young people of his generation had been smitten, as he was, by Jacques Cousteau's passion for his explorations under the sea.

In an interview with David Frost on public television, Jacques Cousteau, at eighty-five, expressed his passionate concern about the future of oceanography, and the future of the planet. This *care* for the planet flowed directly out of his study of the oceans. His particularity had become a universality. This is what so often happens to people who are aging well and who have become truly generative.

The Ericksons tell us that the human strength and virtue that arises out of bearing the tension in our lives between generativity and stagnation is Care. Cousteau told the story of his life. He had been in the navy for twenty-seven years. He said that during all those years, he traveled over so many fascinating oceans and seas always wondering what it was like beneath them. His life, after he retired from the navy, was given to that exploration. Oceanography was then his second, midlife career! He called the depths "a natural, friendly place." He was still diving at eighty-five.

His dream for the future was to build a brand new ship for underwater exploration that he had designed. It would incorporate all the latest technology, including an on-board television production studio hooked up to a satellite in space. This would make live broadcasting of the underwater world possible. His new ship, the *Calypso II*, will have accommodations for men, women, and children. He wanted to sell shares in it to the people of the world so that it will be owned, not by a few rich backers but by ordinary people. This world citizen, born in 1910, spoke with eloquent earnestness about our need for preparing for the more than doubling of the world population to 10 billion people by 2040. He warned, "Only if we begin now to stop wasting the resources of the planet will we survive." He was optimistic however, that we can and will.

His spirit shone through as he reverently, enthusiastically spoke of the awesome beauty, "the sinlessness," of Antarctica, the breathtaking wonder of the Amazon forest that is under ten meters of water. Diving there, he told us, he saw the "interplay of the earth and the water, the yellow dolphins swimming through the inundated trees." His own awesome inner beauty was tangible, is again tangible as I write these words now. We knew that he was sharing his own life's myth of meaning. He was *showing us* his tangible love for the earth. Here was a man who had beheld with his own eyes unfathomable wonders and secrets of our home planet and these visions were transfiguring him in the telling of them. We knew already that we were participating in his prayer of contemplation. However, he went on to make our perception about the subtle inner dimension of this television interview quite concrete.

He talked about his belief in God; about his cultivated, "though not too cultivated," garden around a chapel where he went to spend whole days, talking to, communing with God. He went on to tell us that he believes we are each an instrument in God's symphony, and that each instrument is crucial to that symphony. Yet, he said, "We know so little of that symphony, only something of this earth's part in it. What of the other planets and the infinite number of suns in the universe; what of their part in the symphony?"

Because of this one man's ceaselessly communicated passion, he had given birth to a whole generation of oceanographers. He has made an inestimable contribution to the knowledge about our planet's seas, its last frontier.

The earth's waters had chosen him both to find and to witness their wonders and their fragility. He had responded in a magnificent way. Jacques Cousteau died two years after this television interview at the age of eighty-seven. His dreams live on enfleshed in and carried on by hosts of younger men and women, inspired by him, scientists of the oceans, and in scores of films and this later interview, a last testament to his life.

Thinking about Cousteau's fabulous response to this urging that he received from his own unconscious depths in the second half of his life made us recall Jesus' parable of the talents from the gospel of Matthew. During twenty-seven years in the navy, Cousteau traveled over so many fascinating seas and "always wondered what was under them." How simply, but how persistently a call to use other gifts and talents comes in midlife! How unaware we are, when we begin to follow a dream, where it will lead us and what a great contribution it will make if we say "yes." "I don't remember when or why but someplace and somewhere, I said 'Yes' to someone," Dag Hammarkjold, one-time secretary general of the

United Nations, says in *Markings,* his always-secret personal spiritual journal, published two years after his death. How unconscious we are that this call is the voice of our Self, our soul, our God. How easy to cop out and say, "Hey, this is my time for me. I'm no underwater person, I'm strictly a sailor." How tempting to fall into stagnation when the cost of generativity can be so high. What a penetrating psychologist of human nature Jesus shows himself to be in the simple story of generativity and stagnation chapter 25 of Matthew's Gospel:

> It will be as when a man who was going on a journey called in his servants and entrusted his possessions to them. To one, he gave five talents; [talent, perhaps a bar of silver or gold of high value] to another, two; to a third, one—to each according to ability. Then, he went away. Immediately the one who had received five talents went and traded with them, and made another five. Likewise, the one who received two made another two. But the servant who received one went off and dug a hole in the ground and buried the master's money.

Jesus goes on to tell how the master on his return rejoiced in the accomplishments of the first two.

> Well done, my good and faithful servant. Since you were faithful in small matters, I will give you great responsibilities. Come share your master's joy." Then, the one who had received the one talent came forward and said, "Master, I knew you were a demanding person, harvesting where *you did not plant* and gathering where *you* did not scatter; so out of fear I went off and buried your talent in the ground. Here it is back." His master said to him in reply, "You wicked, lazy servant! *So you knew* that I harvest where I did not plant and gather where I did not scatter? Should you not then have put my money in the bank so that I could have got it back with interest on my return? Now then! Take the talent from him and give it to the one with the ten. For every one who has, more will be given and that one will grow rich; but from the one who has not, even what he or she has will be taken away" (Matthew 25: 14–18, 21–29; *italics ours*).

Each and all of the three who had absolutely nothing of their own are filled to the brim. They have each received up to capacity. Each receives according to ability. Each knows the way, because each knows what the master does—reaps where he did not sow, collects what he did not scatter. We are all in the same position. We all reap what we really did not sow and collect what we really did not scatter. We come into the world that is here before we come, and will be here after us. All is gift. We use what we are given to increase the gift for our own joy, the joy of those around us, and for those who come after us. When we are given new levels of perception and power, we have new obligations. If like the servant we fail to discharge this new responsibility in the right way there is a chance that it will be taken from us. To whom much is given, of that one much will be expected. However, if we fear, and are controlled by it, if we let fear possess us, we have lost sight of both the *Gift* that is ours and the Giver who is always giving it. The gift is our uniqueness and our unique place in the universe, our instrument, our notes in the symphony of the universe.

It is no accident that what follows immediately on this section of chapter 25 in Matthew's gospel is the dramatic separation of the sheep from the goats. Then the king will say to those on his right, "Come here, you blessed of my Father, inherit the kingdom prepared for you from the beginning of the world. After all, I was hungry and you gave me something to eat; thirsty and you gave me something to drink; I was homeless and you took me in; naked and you clothed me; sick and you looked after me; in jail and you came to see me. Then they will ask, 'When Lord, did we see you starving, thirsty, homeless, naked?' And the king will answer, "However much you did do it for any of the least important brothers and sisters of mine, you did it for me." And to those on the left, "Away from me. . . . Howsoever much you did not do for any of those you saw to be the least important people, you wouldn't do it for me either" (Matthew 25: 34–45).

Buddha, having received the supreme gift—his enlightenment—under the Bodhi tree, knew that he could not stay there. He was called to share what he had received. Giving, passing on, circulating the gift is the only way to keep it. One of the most significant spiritual movements of the modern era, Alcoholics Anonymous, has embodied this ancient spiritual truth in the twelfth step of the Twelve Step Program that it has passed on to animate all the other self-help groups which are its spin-offs. Step Twelve: "Having had a spiritual awakening as the result of these steps, we tried to carry this message to alcoholics, and to practice these principles in all our affairs."

We rarely believe how significant our own small gifts are. That is because we do not remember that those gifts are ultimately God's and that our creativity, generativity, and generosity and compassion are ultimately God's.

Rose shared with us a newspaper article about her later-life sharing of her gifts. Rose was an administrator for many years. Earlier in life she had been a domestic arts teacher. When she retired at nearly seventy, Rose found herself plagued by visions of the homeless of Los Angeles. Up from her depths came a call to do something about this situation. She knew her gifts, she knew her experience both as administrator and teacher. She felt the fear that she was too old to start anything new. She felt the self-doubt that she would be able to do anything effective. Yet she went to work. She took her talents and multiplied them. Eventually, Rose opened a soup kitchen to feed the hungry homeless and, undoubtedly, her *own* hunger for meaning and generativity in these later years. This was no ordinary soup kitchen. Rose's place was called, *Bread and Rose's Cafe.* She shared her dream with other dreamers, homeless and not. They all went to work. This cafe for the homeless had donated tablecloths and fresh flowers on the tables. The homeless were trained in the dining room, the pantry, and the kitchen. They trained until they became proficient maitre d's, waiters and waitresses, bussers, dish washers, cooks and cook's helpers; they learned menu making, pricing, and accounting and a host of other things like teamwork and sweeping up, decorating, and bathroom cleaning.

For this cafe, the homeless made reservations. They found themselves treated like guests here. The turnover in help at Bread and Rose's Cafe is great however, as one after another, the homeless are job trained and find—with all other kinds of volunteer help in preparing job applications and interviews—a paying job of their own.

In the first chapter of this book we told the story of Martha Graham's second half of life generativity. She opened the Martha Graham School of Dance as a direct result of her own close encounter with death when all meaning went out of her life as she realized that she could not dance any more. In her autobiography, Martha reveals something of the rhythm of spirit receiving, and spirit giving that we saw in Jacques Cousteau and our friend Rose—to say nothing of Hammarskjold, Buddha, Bill W. of AA, and of course, Jesus of Nazareth. Written late in her long life, this book reveals the same poetic, struggling soul that we saw in her dance and continue to see now in her choreography.

Until her death at ninety-seven, Martha was actively teaching new dancers, generating and teaching new dances for them to perform. There were the many dancers to whom she taught the techniques that she had first evolved in her own body. When she was in her seventies, eighties, and nineties, *no longer able to create on her own body,* she had to *reach within* to find the way to create on other dancers' bodies. The struggle for her was great because her care was not only for a unique physical form and style but for another mystical dimension of this art. She was concerned lest the mythology and transcendent spirit be lost.

She writes in her autobiography, *Blood Memory,* finished the year before she died: "Each day of rehearsal for a new ballet, I arrive a little before two in the afternoon, and sit alone in my studio to have a moment of stillness before the dancers enter. I tease myself and say I am cultivating my Buddha nature; but it is really just a comforting place for me to be—secure, clear and with a purpose. It is the order of these elements together that led one writer to call dance, 'glorified human behavior.' I sit with my back to our large mirrors so that I am completely within myself. . . . You must keep your vessel clean, your mind, your body. It is so easy to become cluttered. I think that is what my father must have meant when he wrote, 'Martha, you must keep an open soul.' It is that openness and awareness, and innocence of sorts that I try to cultivate in my dancers. As our rehearsal begins, I will mention that sensitivity and openness."(6).

She hoped each new ballet she created, and each revival would be an expression of the landscape of the soul. "I hope that every dance I do reveals something of myself or some wonderful thing a human being can be" (6). She felt that each person was born with genius and by genius she meant, "that curiosity that leads to the secret of life." It was her goal to spark that genius in each of her dancers and in each member of their audience. She saw the body as a sacred garment, our first and last. She thought that it should be treated with honor, joy, fear, and always blessing.

Here, like Cousteau in his interview, she shares something of her soul. She is receiving. She opens her spirit to moments of contemplative solitude, her "Buddha nature," she calls it. She spends time alone in her dance studio. She feeds her soul in drinking in the place that is such a comfort to her. It is, she tells us, both a place of sacred fire and a holy well. She feels that the studio is filled with the fire of the energy of her own and generations of dancers. Rudolf Nureyev, Margot Fonteyn, and Mikhail Breshnikov had danced there in that space. Hundreds of others had executed a leap or an arm ripple with a strength or a mystical grace or a presence that had made her heart and the hearts of other observers stand still. Moments of participation in such beauty are peak experiences, religious experiences, a prayer of contemplation.

She wrote that this studio in New York City was built on property where a creek once flowed. She says, "I believe the land still holds some of that hidden water. . . . It is a strange force that seems alive under the building. Even in the studio, we have had a little shoot of plant life come up out of the floor, just near the piano. It is another world and we accept the gift" (8).

Like Cousteau's chapel garden, this is Martha's holy well. It is a place where she can withdraw into herself and center herself, commune with herself, be entirely at home with herself. It was undoubtedly a wellspring of her creativity, and self-creation. Like her, each of us needs to find our own sacred places—places and times that nourish us. We need to retreat to them often if we are to maintain the balance between generativity and stagnation.

There are sacred places all over the earth. Often cathedrals were built over places made sacred by ancient pilgrimages that had already hallowed the place. Entering a cathedral or even a tiny chapel can move us into another dimension of ourselves. Yet, such sacred places can also be as common and accessible as a favorite chair in a tiny corner of our own home, a garden patch, a porch, an ancient tree, a park, a lake or an ocean. We can fill our surroundings with objects that nourish our souls and remove things that clutter our lives and drain our energy.

Martha Graham continued to give her gift until her death in her late nineties. It was only in her sixties that she was able to choreograph for dancers other than herself. At ninety-one she told Betty Friedan in an interview for Betty's monumental book, *The Fountani of Age,* "The body is your instrument in dance, but your art is outside of that creature. I don't leap or primp anymore. I look at young dancers, and I am envious and more than ever aware of what glories the body contains. But sensitivity is not made dull by age" (609). At ninety-six, a few months before her death, she premiered not only a new dance, but something much more playful, something close to jazz, a kind of dance she had never done before! Sensitivity is not made dull by age, nor is creativity or passion for life.

It was out of that ongoing sensitivity that she generated twelve new ballets and scores of revivals right up to the end of her life. In *The Power of Myth* television series, Joseph Campbell showed film clips of individuals who are key to our modern civilization. They are Gandhi, Martin Luther King, Mother Teresa, and Martha Graham, dancing her own ballet, *Lamentations.* She ranks with a handful of recent artists who broke traditional molds and created new forms of expression, changing the way we look at the world. In those last years, she received a Lifetime Achievement award from a grateful country at the Kennedy Center in Washington, D.C. Present at the ceremony, she stood up tall in her box above the audience of dignitaries and bowed with a grace that was a reminder of who this woman was.

The poet May Sarton expresses the power of later life that we saw in Martha Graham when she wrote in her eightieth year in *Encore:*

> These are not hours of fire but years of praise
> The glass full to the brim, completely full
> But held in balance so no drop can spill.

A kind of praise rises out of the movement to wholeness that is this truly generative time of life. The process of individuation, of becoming more whole, of becoming one's true Self no matter what the flaws remaining, just naturally overflows. This kind of generativity, self-giving is only possible when the self has acquired length of days. These people whose stories we are telling could not have given these particular gifts to humanity earlier in their lives since these are the gifts of experience and who these people were now in their later lives.

Of course, the Martha Graham story opens the whole question of finding meaningful work, productivity, and creativity right to the end of our lives. It is not necessary to die with "one's boots on" to do this. Only some of us in some few professions can continue to engage in them into late old age as Martha did. Yet her story of finding a way to do this is a wonderful example of making the compromises necessary to carry on being generative in whatever way we can at each moment of our lives.

Former President Jimmy Carter is another person who found the ways to continue using his talents and life experiences to continue being generative and spirit giving, as well as to engage in his own soul making.

When Carter lost his run for a second term in office, he was "grieved, disappointed and embarrassed." He and Rosalynn, his wife, had to work through a certain amount of bitterness. They could have gone on instead, letting that bitterness grow and consume them. There are many people whose failures or perceived failures and injustices in life cause them to die as sullen, bitter, angry, cantankerous, self-absorbed, old people.

Added to the disgrace of defeat, about two weeks after they were home in Plains, Georgia, they found out to their amazement that they were over a million dollars in debt. The family business had suffered enormous setbacks. They had never been in debt before, so this was an added devastating blow. However, they set about healing their angry, disappointed, pained hearts. This took no small effort. In many ways, the books they wrote after that time chronicle their growing strength and complete turnabout. In large part, the authoring helped pay off the debt. Thus, it is possible that the world would be bereft of some enormously valuable documents of monumental second half of life growth if the Carters had never gotten into debt! Eventually, they organized the Carter Center.

The Carter Center is involved in monitoring and analyzing all the conflicts and wars going on in the world. Yet the conflict resolution part of the center is about 10 percent of its total commitment. The Center has twenty-six to forty different health programs. It has at least 150,000 small farmers in Africa whom they are teaching how to grow more grain to help alleviate starvation, along with many other like programs.

In analyzing each war going on in the world, the Carter Center because it is a private, not a government agency can and does analyze, in a completely unofficial way, both sides of the conflict. There is an objectivity possible because the grievances of the side *not supported by America* are understood as completely as the United States' favored side.

In an interview with Charlie Rose, remarkable Public Television interviewer, Carter said,

> We try to understand the basic causes of the war, or the conflict, or the revolution, or the human rights abuses. And we try to understand not just one side but both sides. When we do get an opportunity to go in and try to resolve a conflict or alleviate suffering, or deal with a human rights or crimes, then we go in trying to address the person who is responsible, or the person who is not ordinarily contacted for cooperation. . . . The main thing I do is listen. . . . I try to be thoroughly briefed about our own U.S. Policy, the policy of the United Nations . . . and I go with the full knowledge and approval, in every case, of my own government, always with the President's approval. In the case of North Korea, I had invitations from the leadership for three solid years. "Please come over here and help me resolve this problem that I have with your country." But for three years, the government didn't want me to go and I didn't go.

When finally Carter did go, he tried, he said, "To use the highest developed science or technique of mediation. Unless both sides win, then any sort of agreement cannot be permanent, anything more than transient."

Carter's interest in peacemaking surely goes back to his own very committed Christian principals. Blessed are the peacemakers, they shall be called children of God. Yet it can also be traced to his presidency when he mediated between Egypt and Israel. It also undoubtedly has some roots in the greatest failure of his presidency, the terrible U.S./Iranian hostage crisis. His inability to resolve this conflict cost him the election.

Growing, individuating, generative, passionate people are able to integrate the joys and sorrows, successes and failures of a life's experiences and transform them into gold. We all need to be alchemists of soul. Emerson once said that we are punished *by* our sins, not for them. This is a profound insight. Yet, even more profound and mysterious is the experience of good and growth that can come out of the evil and failure, yes, even sins of our life. Grieved, mourned, they can be the source of abundant life. Remorse can be a powerful energy as long as we do not identify with it. Out of death comes new life. The inner meaning of the resurrection of Jesus is just this. Christians call it the Paschal Mystery. In an ancient Christian hymn, the Exultet, sung at the vigil of Easter, the exuberant, rejoicing Church calls the sin of Adam and Eve, and so the sin of humanity, a *happy fault* because it "won for us so great a Savior." How radical this really is. Yet who of us has not experienced that some of our greatest strength and best qualities have grown in the soil of our greatest pain, or evil and the evil done against us. What is incomprehensible on the rational level is profoundly true on the level of soul.

In Jimmy Carter the uses of defeat, failure, financial disaster, and even ongoing criticism and misunderstanding are obvious. Who is to say that he could have done as much if he had served another term as president.

At the end of this interview with Jimmy Carter in his seventies, Carter said, "I think, if I had to make a judgment, now is the best time of my life." When the interviewer asked, "Why?" He answered, "It's about grandchildren and my wife, Rosalynn, and I being home in Plains, Georgia, and being financially stable, primarily because of the success of the books I've written. The Carter Center's work is so diverse that we can do several different things every day that are challenging and interesting. There's a thing about having been President of the greatest nation on earth, and that is that I have access to almost any person in the world, and if I want to write somebody, they answer my letter. If I go visit perpetrators of human rights abuses and express my concern, they are quite likely to do something to alleviate the human rights concerns that we have. So it makes it easy for me to be influential, having been President of the United States."

If retired government officials or each retired celebrity were to find such creative ways to use their celebrity to continue to contribute, the impact on the world would be enormous. This is an example of a modern adaptation of the role of elder among ancient peoples as the ideal mediator. The elder was the one who could transcend personal interest, having moved beyond power struggles of youth.

When the Wise Old Man and Wise Old Women Archetype rises in a person it gives great insight into things that move people. Such a person can really listen, get out of the way and make space within for another's point of view. One feels really listened to by this kind of being heard. The agendas of the listener are not a source of static interference as they can be in so many conversations between peers. One is honored by having been heard and taken seriously by the Wisdom figure. There is a kind of universality about the Sage. His or her world transcends petty concerns. The goal of the Sage is the genuine good and growth of each individual, the care of the earth, the universe, the things of the soul and the spirit.

Yet the Wise Old Man, Wise Old Woman Archetype are within every human person. Sometimes we have even seen it rise in a child and people say, "Out of the mouths of babes." We are usually not too aware of this wisdom figure within because we project it outside of ourselves and find our wisdom figures in the world outside. Yet within each of us is that source of Wisdom that guides our own lives. That Wisdom comes fleeting in and out of our consciousness. If we are aging well, we are becoming more and more permeable to its influence.

It is the Spirit of Wisdom that guides us to and through our unique role in the intricate web of the whole human story and project. At the core of the archetype is something far greater than it. There is Something that the Hebrew Scripture calls *Ruah,* the Spirit, the breath of God. There is Something that they called *Sophia,* Holy Wisdom "From the mouth of the Most High I came forth, and mist-like covered the earth. In the highest heavens did I dwell, My throne on a pillar of cloud. . . . Come to me all you that yearn for me. . . . The first man and woman never finished comprehending Wisdom nor will the last succeed in fathoming her. For deeper than the sea are her thoughts; her counsels, than the great abyss" (Sirach 24).

Wisdom and age are associated. Our life experience opens us to see and know more than we ever knew before. "If only I knew then what I know now," we find ourselves thinking. There is a space now opening onto the bigger picture, ego is a little more out of the way. Our new vulnerability leaves room for Wisdom to come into our house. There is a lovely old saying, *"too soon old, too late wise."* There is an ancient prayer based on the psalms that seems to suit very well the inner cry for wisdom of the second half of life. It is this:

> Come, Holy Spirit, fill the hearts of your faithful
> And kindle in them the fire of your divine Love
> Send forth your Spirit and we shall be recreated
> And You shall renew the face of the earth.

In youth, we thought it was we who would renew the face of the earth. Now that we *know* it is God who will do it, we have paradoxically a real possibility of getting somewhere. Witness Jimmy Carter and our friend, Peter Bosset.

Peter Bosset retired from his job in a brewery at sixty-five. Shortly after his retirement, the county began plans to build a senior citizen apartment house on the next block. His neighborhood started to change from a predominantly Irish/Italian to a primarily African-American one. Peter made friends with his new neighbors. Never before political in any way, he became vice president of his block association in an integrating neighborhood where he remained while many of his white neighbors moved away. He and his neighbors organized and fought to transform a proposed high-rise senior residence into a beautiful, five-story patio-faced building surrounded by a large grassy lawn, with plenty of space for the seniors' vegetable gardens.

Peter began to volunteer every Wednesday at a local hospital. He was always offering a hand to neighbors, sweeping, shoveling, even washing cars. He had been a good husband and father. Now he took over much of the shopping for his wife and was out every cold morning moving cars in his driveway so that his daughter could get off to work. He became a very attentive grandfather.

Eventually, Peter learned that a local food bank needed a driver and he offered his services. Then, for ten years, until his final illness, Peter was out at 7:00 A.M. every morning, except Wednesday, which he reserved for hospital volunteer work. He went every day to pick up food from churches, synagogues, and other collection agencies of Newark, New Jersey, and then, deliver it to the needy.

He enlisted the help of relatives and friends to provide for special needs of special groups. One of his pet causes was a residence for babies with AIDS.

In these years, whenever Peter spoke about anyone he met on his rounds, he would call the person, "a wonderful man . . . a wonderful woman." He always saw the *more* in people. The day before he died of cancer, Pete was all excited about the Rabbi. "He's a wonderful man." The Rabbi visited him in the hospital and told Pete that he had just collected $5,000 for the food bank.

Peter's wake and funeral were enormous gatherings of "wonderful men and women," black, white, Hispanic, Asian, the very rich and very poor, the very simple, the unkempt, the very educated and the well-dressed. They were brought together, sincerely grieved at his sudden death, and one after another telling stories of amazing, ingenuous acts of love and kindness. There were tales, as well, of a gentle wisdom. It is easy to believe that Pete the brewery worker of earlier days would have been as surprised by it all as were some of his former neighbors who traveled back to the old neighborhood for Pete's wake, and relatives who came from a distance. One does not have to be a former President to bring together those who are strangers to one another or to make a significant difference. Being vice president of a block association, or a driver for a food pantry, will do.

Generativity and creativity takes even much more simple forms than this. Marie was in her late eighties. She was in rather poor health but she could still knit. Everyone that she knew got something warm for Christmas every year. More than that they got the warmth of her unconditional love and mothering, an Irish hospitality, a kind word, and an honest concern. Moreover there was always the heartening promise of a Rosary said "for your intentions."

Tom and Betty found a book on spirituality and psychology of midlife, which they enjoyed and found a great help. Realizing that many of their friends were in midlife, they decided to pass on the book. Eventually, when several others had read it, they decided to get together to discuss it. This led to a full-range book discussion group on the issues involved. Eventually, this led to their attending a workshop that was led by the authors. After this, they invited the authors to conduct a workshop for their group and opened it to a large group of interested people in the Washington, D.C., area. This was how we met Tom and Betty. After that Tom and Betty ran other workshops where we were invited to be the presenters and continued to lead other book discussion groups for many midlife people. How simply something begins. Book discussion groups are a way that many older adults have found, not only as a way to go on learning but as a way to share the immense wealth of their years of learning through their own real-life experience with others.

A husband and wife team, both brain scientists in their sixties, are doing some important research on Alzheimer's Disease together. They have found that learning something entirely new is a way of keeping the brain stimulated, and thus, they believe, preventing Alzheimer's and other loss of brain power. As busy as they are with their research, they have decided to learn something entirely new themselves. They are both learning how to sculpt as a whole new avenue for their creativity and a stimulation for their brains.

Mary McKeon was in her seventies when she came to the first Mid-Life Directions Workshop that we ever facilitated. In fact, Mary's workshop predates the name Mid-Life Directions. Mary was one of twenty-four people. Together with this group we launched, unknown to us at the time what was to become our new life's work. Mary hated to see this experience end. She was at the time caring for an invalid husband, and this was a special and stimulating opportunity to be with other adults, talking about important things. The dynamism that was to launch the second career of each of us was palpable in the energy of those eight meetings with those twenty-three-, forty- or fifty-something-year-olds and Mary. So much so, that half the group continued to go on meeting because Mary spearheaded those meetings in the beginning. A retired teacher, she decided after her husband's death to return to school. She earned a masters in theology and began to teach adult education courses in a religious education center. She continued that, as well as her meetings with her Mid-Life Directions group until her death some ten years later. It was to Mary that we owe the fact that we have always advertised our Mid-Life Directions Workshops for men and women "35–65 +." It was to Mary that we owe the fact that very early on, we started offering Long Life Directions Workshops, again predating the name, to people 60–85 +. It was Mary who first taught us about the similarities as well as the differences in the different decades of the second half of life. It was Mary who first showed us how growth and personality development go on primarily through a person's own inner environment in the second half of life. From the day she read an announcement about a midlife workshop and decided that she would not pay attention to the culture outside her that said "you're too old," to the initiative she took to ask her group if they wanted to go on meeting; to ignoring the voices that told her a degree at her age would be a waste of time and money, she followed the directions of an individuating inner Self. It was Mary who first taught us about the new phenomenon of the Young Old. What was old, fifty years ago, is not old now. Anyone who doesn't believe that just needs to spend some time with some nearby eighty-year olds. There are Mary McKeons all over the place. Contrary to popular misconceptions, only a small percentage of the elderly ever live in nursing homes. While in the 1950s these few were moving in at sixty-five, today these residents are moving to nursing homes in their eighties.

The intellectual ravages of aging are another misconception. Only ten percent of people in their seventies ever develop dementia. Much of the mental decline that we have formerly associated with age is in fact proving to be caused by treatable medical problems such as hypertension, prescription drug reactions, diabetes, and depression. Changes in diet and exercise, the relief of poverty (which is not a healthy lifestyle), and advances in medicine are all helping to create the age evolution that we have been talking about in this book. When death does come and those final illnesses that lead to it, they are more and more frequently coming to people who like Mary have lived the fullness of life, draining joy and sufferings to the last drop, and struggling to remain fully alive even in dying. To quote Carl Jung again, "I have treated many old people [he was in his eighties when he said this] and when the unconscious is apparently threatened with the complete end, it ignores it. Life behaves as if it were going on. So I tell old people to live on as though they had centuries and then they will live properly." The great religious stories about life after death, eternal life, touch this same mystery and paradox: Life goes on even after death. These beliefs touch the core of our humanity. "If for this life only we have hoped in Christ, we are of all people most to be pitied," says Saint Paul to the Corinthians who are denying that their dead live on. Paul goes on, "But in fact Christ has been raised from the dead, the first fruits of those who have fallen asleep" (1 Cor. 19–20). Live on as though you have eternal life and then you will live properly. Live with a passion for life for ultimately, life is eternal and your passion is for *eternal life* and the living God.

Grandparenting

It was very significant that in the interview with Jimmy Carter that we talked about earlier, Carter when asked why he said that this was the best time of his life, first mentioned his wife, Roslyn, and then his grandchildren. This came before all his discussion of the incredible fruitfulness of his work at the Carter Center, his many books, his work as statesman.

A grandchild is an unspeakably awesome accomplishment. It is a fulfillment of one's being and *being here,* at a time when one is ready to appreciate the mystery of it. Grandparenting well is generativity par excellence. It carves the strength that is care deeply in one's being. For so many women and men, grandparenting elicits a kind of nurturing of one's children's children that was not possible with one's own children. A person gets another chance to do it. But more, one gets a chance when one has the wisdom, experience and patience that were not possible in youth. In youth, we were simply incapable of being this experienced, of having this insight about who this little human being really is. After all, we have known her great grandparents and maybe even her great, great grandparents. We can see them clearly, remember their laughter, hear their voices, recall angry and joking moments, tell a story they always told, using most of their lines. We see or hear them now alive again in this child's smile or nose, a gift for music or in the twinkle of an eye.

We were there at this baby's mother's birth, or the father's birth. We hear her mother or father in her cries, we see her mother in her tiny face and stance and in her stubborn, abrupt refusals, her chin at the exact same angle. We know this child, and know about her, as only a grandparent who sees her in this larger context can know. This, of course if we are a grandparent who has grown in consciousness ourselves. If we have learned to see beneath the surface of things to their inner dimensions, if we can see the deep down things. We are more aware if our ego is out of the way. We see the more if we are no longer egocentric, if we are not filled with blindspots because we are still projecting all our negative shadows on the world around us. We see the *more* after we have gotten through the initial shock of being old enough to be a grandparent.

As I was writing this, I read a letter in a newspaper from a daughter whose mother was not a nurturing grandmother. The letter writer said that her mother was in good health when her father died and could have lived in her own apartment. Yet she insisted that she needed someone to take care of her, and announced that she was coming to live with her daughter, her husband, and grandchildren. "Period!" It had to be the daughter, even though she worked full time because she certainly could not interfere with her "son's career goals." However, grandma told her son-in-law that they could buy a pull-out sofa for himself and her daughter and then she could move into their bedroom. Naturally, mom casually let it drop that the children would have to give up their noisy piano, horn, and dance lessons. Mother certainly could not be expected to endure the noise of their rowdy friends or her son-in-law's boisterous friends either. She also made it clear that any evening socializing had to end at 9:00 P.M., everyone should be in bed by then anyway, because once awakened she would never get back to sleep again. This certainly meant early supper and no late afternoon activities for the kids and probably no entertaining for anyone.

Here is an egocentric grandmother who is indeed not a grandmother in any real sense of the word. She obviously has never made a midlife transition, or she has totally regressed; her ego is still the center of her universe. She is blind to her shadow of selfishness. She has not really, consciously let her daughter "grow up and leave home." She is oblivious of her son-in-law, of the needs and reality of her grandchildren. She has not grown in awareness, in consciousness, in soulfulness. She is a one-dimensional, myopic, paper, mostly dead person. Reading her story we know that she is not one of a kind. Her picture makes the contrast between herself and an individuating, growing, contemplating conscious grandparent, stand out in greater relief.

Recently, I said to a group of grandmothers, "You know, I think that I miss not being a grandmother far more than I missed being a mother." Spontaneously, three of them said, "You should!" This time around, they said, one gets the chance to nurture without the twenty-four-hour responsibility for the life of a child that is a parent's. As most grandparents are able to say, "These kids go home!"

Grandparents can show supportive concern in a more relaxed objective way than they could when they were harried parents. They can listen to the child with new ears and hear at deeper levels. They know the pain, they have been there but they know what heals as well. They can give the child entry to another world, another time. Their stories of "back then before computers and maybe even TV" are as magical and soul feeding as fairy tales and myths. They give the child a new set of eyes, a heart, and a perspective otherwise lost to him or her. When grandparents see their own brown eyes looking back at them or their own grandmother's nose or sense of humor in their grandchild they are loving that child in a transcendent way, no matter what the child's flaws.

They have the perspective to know that this clumsy time, or this bad habit too will pass. They have been here before. They can take things more calmly. They can give a freedom to the child to be who he or she is. They can really play with a child; really teach them to draw, wield a hammer, or fix a car.

Grandparents like this, unlike the Scrooge-hearted woman of the story above, have gotten out of their own way. As one grandparents, one is often simultaneously renewing and repairing relationships with one's own grown sons and daughters by supporting them in their difficult roles. There is so much personality development that can happen through all this. One begins to change one's way of being with other people and seeing things about one's past parenting that one never saw before.

Phil, a man in his fifties, always a career-oriented father, had not been there very often when his own four children were being reared. Now he is to his seven grandchildren the father that he never was to his own children. He loves to be with them, even though he is still very involved in the ups and downs of his own business and is traveling frequently. He takes every opportunity to spend hours with the children. He takes two- and four-year-olds off alone to the circus or the petting zoo; something he would never have attempted in the macho days of his youth. He is constantly telling stories about each one with a relish and detail that reveal each individual child's personality. He is always taking pictures of them and videoing them. He basks in their obvious affection for him. In the process, he is developing a whole other feeling and compassionate side of his personality. His family and friends see the difference, the new richness in him. Always a lovable, exciting person, he has a new depth. Not long ago, having just spent a day with his daughter, her very involved-in-fathering young husband and their two babies, he had a catch in his throat, as he talked about his wife of thirty-five years, and asked for the first time how she managed with *four* children.

A grandmother, mother of four herself, recently told me that being present at the birth of her daughter's first child was one of the most sacred experiences of her life.

A grandmother of three two-year-olds, recently recycled all the old toys from her attic and purchased some new stuff at a series of garage sales to make her beautiful new home more child-friendly again. She has tremendous sensitivity to the style of parenting of each of her adult children and following their lead can move from one grandson to the other with extraordinary versatility. At the same time she delights in the uniqueness of each little boy and is an extraordinarily keen forecaster of their needs and whims. She is adjusting, like so many modern grandmothers, to the vastly different lifestyles of these new parents: the full-time mother, the divorced father, the career mother. There is more to her own life than her grandchidren. She does not try, or need to live through them. Yet, she is willing to make profound sacrifices to be there for them.

Another grandfather said, "I was never someone who thought about the future of the country, the future of the earth. The rhetoric of those who did fell on deaf ears with me until . . . until I saw my first grandchild. I do recycle now. I do make noise about the way things are going on the national and the international level."

As a final story of how the generativity that is grandfathering and grandmothering brings about growth not only in the child, but the next generations, but growth and passion for life in the grandparents, we want to let one grandfather speak for himself. A social worker and federal parole officer, Kevin Danaher, wrote a story, "The Magic Dot" about his two-year-old granddaughter. She was his first grandchild. We quote from his as yet unpublished manuscript (by permission):

THE MAGIC DOT

Once upon a time toward the end of the 20th Century a princess was born. Although only a very few knew of her princess-ness, most who met her recognized she was a very special little girl with very special and very unusual qualities.

For instance, when the music plays (although she has her favorites almost any music will do) she can mesmerize a crowd large or small, friends, or strangers, As a matter of fact she dances in such a way as to seem oblivious to being the center of riveted attention. But enough, that's only an aside.

As of this recording, the princess is almost two but she has from the first had a most captivating way with those very close to her including her grandfather. I use him as an example simply because he, I suppose like many of us, is a worrier. He often frets and loses sleep about things over which he has absolutely no control, like the affairs of yesterday, or the next hour, or the next week, or the next ten years, or—well you get the idea. Anyway, when he is with the princess all this changes. He is very different then. You see, the princess is not one to worry about all these things, or to worry at all for that matter. She is much too busy being involved in the affairs of the present and she forces her grandfather to do the same. For instance, when visiting she often takes him by the finger to walk from the front deck to the back deck, a distance of some fifty feet which he ordinarily covers in about ten seconds, but one that now can take five minutes or ten or even more. First she has to be lifted up to see if any bees are at work in the "blue bell" flowers. If so, then her grandfather is in for a long hold. Eventually, the two saunter down the side deck stopping every few feet to look over the wooden railing into the side yard for a cat, or a dog, or a bird, or a squirrel. Any positive sightings will of course add to the length of the trip. When the back deck is finally reached, the Princess Wagon (oddly enough sold in Toys-Are-Us with many common wagons) comes into view and herself quickly makes it clear that it is time for a royal ride. Bear in mind she is not yet able to talk, which forces her grandfather, and anyone else who takes the time to listen, to concentrate all his faculties in an attempt to understand her. This has the effect of forcing him to be in the world of the princess that is always the here and now. One can't possibly do otherwise for fear of offending or frustrating royalty. And so after awhile, and some believe the grandfather may have been the first to understand what others flippantly term baby talk or gibberish, he knew what sounds and gestures meant bird or cat or plane or bug, or cassette player or pretzel or whatever. How could he possibly, during these adventures and conversations, have any time for his traditional concerns? It is for him, as it would be for anyone in such a situation, impossible. And mind you, in all this the princess never resorts to extraordinary means. She points out and speaks about and laughs at the most ordinary things. Without revealing all of the exploits of such a one, the chronicler would like to share but one example that has a way of uncovering perhaps as none other the secret of life revealed by the princess, the secret revealed in the Magic Dot.

About halfway through the short life of the princess—the writer believes she waited only so her grandfather would be better prepared to accept the secret—she introduced him to the Magic Dot. Now to the untrained eye the Dot looks ordinary enough and actually could be mistaken for a flat circular piece of paper about one-quarter inch in diameter, much like the product of a simple hole punch. Anyway, soon after showing this Magic Dot to her grandfather the two could often be heard in raucous laughter in the back room. Closer investigation would find the two flat on the lineoleum floor blowing the Dot from one end of the room to the other. From time to time on the intitiative of the princess herself the Dot is moved to the arm of the couch where with uncanny accuracy she, with one short puff, propels it to the solid blue pillow being ceremoniously held by her grandfather much, one suspects, as he would hold the pillow for her jeweled diadem had she chosen to wear one. Then it is the grandfather's ritual duty to stand and blow once so the princess can oh and ah as the Dot gently flutters to the floor. Touchdown is the signal for both to fall to the floor where the huffing and puffing begins anew.

This game, or rather this lesson, continues until such time as the princess apparently believes her grandfather's lesson has gone on long enough or decides it's time for a dance with her grandfather who seems to find it impossible to turn down such a request, especially for a waltz or an Irish jig. Or maybe the princess realizes at some point that at her grandfather's age bouncing on the bare floor is not so easy. Whatever prompts her timing to stop or interrupt the Magic Dot lesson, she undoubtedly balances this with his need, which she intuitively understands, to stop and blow the Magic Dot.

This writer has had the unique privilege of witnessing the ritual of the Magic Dot and can attest first-hand that the secret of life lies therein. The princess knows only one way to live: to embrace, celebrate, and rejoice in the present moment. She is patiently impressing this lesson on her grandfather. He on the other hand, is slowly accepting what she has always known as truth. It seems odd now, but for a while he actually believed he would be the teacher, revealing to her all he had learned about life. Instead, he is ever so slowly coming to realize that the princess is teaching him, much like his first princess tried to do about thirty years ago at a time he was too busy being her father. Now, thankfully, he has more time and maybe more understanding and hopefully can learn what he himself must at one time have known but so long ago forgotten.

And so we come in the second half of life back to the place where we began and now know it really for the first time. We meet the Child in ourselves again and s/he leads us to passion for life.

Bibliography for Notes
and Suggested Readings

Benson, M.D., Herbert. *Timeless Healing*. New York: A Fireside Book-Simon & Shuster, 1996

Blass, Bill in interview with Charlie Rose, Transcript #1078. March 22, 1994. Denver, Colorado, Journal Graphics, Thirteen/WNET

Bolles, Richard. *The Three Boxes of Life: And How to Get Out of Them*. Berkeley, Calif.: Ten Speed Press, 1978

Borg, Marcus, Editor. *Jesus and Buddha: The Parallel Sayings*. Berkeley, Calif.: Ulysses Press, 1997

Brennan, Anne and Brewi, Janice. *Mid-Life Directions: Praying and Playing Sources of New Dynamism*. New York: Paulist Press, 1985

Brewi, Janice and Brennan, Anne. *Celebrate Mid-Life: Jungian Archetypes and Mid-Life Spirituality*. New York: Crossroad, 1988. Revised: *Mid-Life Spirituality and Jungian Archetypes*. Yorktown, Maine: Nicholas-Hayes, 1999

Brewi, Janice and Brennan, Anne. *Mid-Life: Psychological and Spiritual Perspectives*. New York: Crossroad, 1982

Brodie, Fawn M. *Thomas Jefferson: An Intimate History*. New York: Bantam Books: 1974

Browning, Robert. "Rabbi ben Ezra." *The Poems*, Volume One. New York: Penguin Books, 1993

Campbell, Joseph and Boa, Fraser. *This Business of the Gods*. (book and film) Caldon East, Ontario, Canada: Windrose Films Ltd., 1989

Campbell, Joseph with Moyers, William. *The Power of Myth*. New York: Doubleday, 1988

Carter, Jimmy. *Always a Reckoning and Other Poems*. New York: Times Books Random House, 1995

Carter, Jimmy in interview with Rose, Charlie, Transcript #1293, January 17, 1995. Denver, Colorado, Journal Graphics, Thirteen/WNET

D'Arcy, Paula. *Gift of the Red Bird: A Spiritual Encounter.* New York: Crossroad, 1997

Danaher, M.S., M.S.W., Kevin. *The Magic Dot* from his unpublished manuscript.

Delany, Sarah L. and Delany, A. Elizabeth with Amy Hill Heath. *Having Our Say: The Delany Sisters First One Hundred Years.* New York: Dell Publishing, 1993

Delany, Sarah L. with Amy Hill Heath. *On My Own at 107: Reflections on Life without Bessie.* New York: Harper Collins Publisher, 1997

Erikson, Erik H. *The Life Cycle Completed.* New York: W. W. Norton and Company, 1982

Erikson, Erik H. and Joan M. and Kiunick, Helen. *Vital Involvement in Old Age.* New York: W. W. Norton & Company, 1986

Erikson, Joan M. *Wisdom and the Senses.* New York: W. W. Norton and Company, 1988

Friedan, Betty. *The Fountain of Age.* New York: Simon and Shuster, 1993

Goleman, Daniel. *Erikson in His Old Age Expands His View of Life. New York Times,* June 1988

Gordon, Mary. *My Mother Is Speaking from the Desert. New York Times Sunday Magazine,* March 19, 1995, pp. 44–70

Graham, Martha. *Blood Memory: An Autobiography.* New York: Doubleday, 1991

Guditus, Peggy. *Kaleidoscope: The Poetry of Peggy Guditus.* Helen Morris, Editor. Stony Brook, New York: Taproot Workshops and Journal, 1997

Hammarskjold, Dag. *Markings.* Translated by Leif Sjoberg and W. H. Auden. New York: Alfred A. Knopf, 1971

Jung, C. G. *Collected Works.* (Bollinger Series XX) 20 vols. Trans. R. F. C. Hull, Ed. H. Read, M. Fordham, G. Adler Wm. McGuire. Princeton: Princeton University Press, (1953–79)

————. *Memories, Dreams, Reflections.* Aniela Jaffe, Editor. New York: Randon House, 1961

————*"The Stages of Life." Modern Man in Search of a Soul.* Translated by W. S. Dell and Cary F. Baynes. New York: Harcourt, Brace and World, Inc., 1933

————. *Two Essays on Analytical Psychology.* (CW7). New Jersey: Princeton University Press, 1966

Kushner, Harold S. *When Bad Things Happen to Good People.* New York: Avon, 1981

Millner, Nancy. *Creative Aging: Discovering the Unexpected Joys of Aging.* San Francisco: Davies Black, 1997

Michener, James A. *The World Is My Home: A Memoir.* New York: Random House, 1992

Moody, Ph.D., Harry and Carroll, David. *The Five Stages of the Soul: Charting the Spiritual Passages That Shape Our Lives.* New York: Doubleday, 1997

Pretat, Jane R. *Coming to Age: The Croning Years and Late Life Transformations.* Toronto: Inner City Books, 1994

Progoff, Ira. *At a Journal Workshop.* New York: Dialogue House, 1975

Quigg, Philip W., Editor. *Taproot: A Journal of Older Writers.* Stony Brook, New York: Taproot Workshops, Inc., Autumn, 1993, Vol. 13, No. 2. Peggy Guditus and other poets

Roszak, Theodore. *America the Wise: The Longevity Revolution and the True Wealth of Nations.* New York: Houghton Mifflin, 1998

Rumi. *"The Guest House." The Essential Rumi.* Translated by Coleman Barks with John Moyne. Ca.: Harper San Francisco, 1995, p. 109

Sarton, May. *Encore: A Journal of the Eightieth Year.* New York: W. W. Norton & Company, 1993

Schachter, Shalomi and Miller, Ronald S. *From Age-ing to Sage-ing.* New York: Warner Books, 1995

Scott-Maxwell, Florida. *The Measure of My Days.* New York: Penguin Books, 1979

Sheehy, Gail. *Pathfinders: Overcoming the Crisis of Adult Life and Finding Your Own Path to Wellbeing.* New York: William Morrow, 1981

Walcott, Derek. *Sea Grapes.* Farrar, Strauss & Giroux, 1976

Woodward, Kenneth L. "Erik Erikson: Teaching Others How to See." *America.* Vol. 171, No. 4, August 13–20, 1994, pp. 6–8

Yeats, William Butler. "Sailing to Byzantium" and "Vacillation." *The Poems of W. B. Yeats:* A New Edition. Richard J. Finneran, Editor. New York: Macmillan Publishing Company, 1961, 1983

Mid-Life Directions

For the Personal and Spiritual Growth of Adults
in Life's Second Half.

An International Not-for-Profit Organization

FOUNDERS-DIRECTORS
DR. ANNE BRENNAN, csj
and DR. JANICE BREWI, csj

WORKSHOPS • RETREATS • SEMINARS

Mid-Life Directions Personal and Spiritual Growth Workshop for People 35–65 +

Long Life Directions Personal and Spiritual Growth Workshop for People 60–70–85 +

Professional Training and Certifying Program to prepare men and women to facilitate Mid-Life/Long Life Directions Programs in their own places of work.

Certified Mid-Life Directions Consultants are found across the United States and Canada, and in Newfoundland, Ireland, England, Rome-Italy, the Philippines, Thailand, Singapore and Malaysia, North India, Zimbabwe-Africa and Kenya-East Africa.

For a calendar of Mid-Life Directions Programs, to sponsor a program or information on the training: SASE

Mid-Life Directions
4 Palm Avenue
Brick, NJ 08723-7222.

About the Authors

Anne Brennan, csj, and Janice Brewi, csj, are the co-founders and directors of Mid-Life Directions for Personal and Spiritual Growth, a not-for-profit organization in Brick, New Jersey, founded in 1981. They are the creators and international facilitators of Mid-Life Directions (35–65 +) and Long Life Directions (60–85 +) workshops, seminars, and retreats. Since 1986, they have been training other professionals to facilitate Mid-Life/Long Life Directions programs in their own places of work. These certified Mid-Life Directions Consultants are found throughout the United States and Canada, in Newfoundland, Ireland, the Philippines, Rome, England, India, Africa, Singapore, Thailand, Malaysia, and Australia. They are the coauthors of three books on Mid-Life:

Mid-Life Psychological and Spiritual Perspectives
Mid-Life Directions: Praying, Playing, and Other Sources of New
   Dynamism
Mid-Life Spirituality and Jungian Archtypes (Nicholas-Hays, 1999)

Both have doctorates and did their studies in Adult Psychological and Spiritual Growth.